6.99

Children
and Angels

Best wishes,

Gwennyo S. LeKordey

D1556622

By the same author

An Angel at my Shoulder
Out of the Blue

Children and Angels

True stories of angelic help in times of trouble

BY GLENNYCE S. ECKERSLEY

RIDER

LONDON • SYDNEY • AUCKLAND • JOHANNESBURG

First published in 1999

1 3 5 7 9 10 8 6 4 2

Copyright © Glennyce S. Eckersley 1999

The right of Glennyce S. Eckersley to be identified as the Author of this work has been asserted by her in accordance with the Copyright, Designs and Patents Act, 1988.

All rights reserved. No part of this publication may be reproduced, stored in a retrieval system, or transmitted in any form or by any means, electronic, mechanical, photocopying, recording or otherwise, without the prior permission of the copyright owner.

Published in 1999 by Rider
an imprint of Ebury Press, Random House
20 Vauxhall Bridge Road, London SW1V 2SA
www.randomhouse.co.uk

Random House Australia (Pty) Limited
20 Alfred Street, Milsons Point, Sydney,
New South Wales 2061, Australia

Random House New Zealand Limited
18 Poland Road, Glenfield,
Auckland 10, New Zealand

Random House South Africa (Pty) Limited
Endulini, 5A Jubilee Road,
Parktown 2193, South Africa

Random House UK Limited Reg. No. 954009

Papers used by Rider are natural, recyclable products made from wood grown in sustainable forests.

Typeset by SX Composing DTP, Rayleigh, Essex
Printed by Cox and Wyman, Reading, Berks.

A CIP catalogue record for this book is available from the British Library

ISBN 0-7126-7077-7

In memory of Daniel Greenberg

The state of little children surpasses the state of all others in that they are in innocence; and in innocence all things of heaven can be implanted, for it is a receptacle of the truth of faith and of the good of love.

Emanuel Swedenborg, *Heaven and Hell*

Contents

Preface

Ever since I first became aware of stories of angelic encounters, the ones involving children have held a special fascination for me. One aspect of this interest is that people who have had experiences in childhood have had a lifetime to look back on what took place, yet the encounter has almost always retained its clarity and wonder. Sometimes it still holds a sense of mystery or of not being fully understood, a state which children are perhaps generally more comfortable in than adults.

The child's experience of life is often full of excitement and enthusiasm. As we grow older we acquire greater knowledge and awareness of complexity, as well as an unwillingness to take things at face value. These are not necessarily wrong, but they often seem to work against many positive childlike qualities, such as the ability to play, trust, and express feelings spontaneously and openly.

Children have a wonderful, unquestioning spirituality; their inner eyes are wide open, enabling them to see what we as adults have lost. It often seems that the more we learn, the less we know. Scepticism, ridicule and peer pressure gradually force us to leave this innocent spirituality behind. Could it be that civilisations follow a similar pattern – the more sophisticated they become the less spiritual? The advanced western societies are delving into ancient eastern religions and the spirituality of indigenous peoples, wishing to absorb some of the wisdom and insight that these traditions still retain.

The philosopher and theologian Emanuel Swedenborg teaches that angels are within. We need not search outside ourselves, we only need to discover what is already within, albeit well hidden. The title of this book brings together two words which often have the adjective 'inner' placed in front of them. Discovering the 'inner child' and 'inner angel' brings us back full circle. As adults we need to relearn what we have known from the beginning but have forgotten along the way.

The meaning of the word 'angel' is messenger. The primary function of angels is to mediate between ourselves and God. They bring us messages of reassurance and love, and the powerful, abiding knowledge that we are never alone. Every religion and every culture has references to these magnificent beings. Many religions teach that we each have our own personal guardian angel, and that children are particularly close to their specially assigned angel. Angels have many functions; they rescue us, comfort us, accompany us to the next world, and activate our 'inner child'. Another theory is that angels were formerly human beings who have now proceeded to the next stage of life to develop as angels. This belief is supported by the many stories of angel encounters as visits from loved ones in angelic form.

It has been a great pleasure whilst researching this book to hold workshops for children and listen to their opinions on angels. Few doubted they had their own guardian angel, or doubted the function of such a being. Clear ideas emerged from even the very youngest children. Children of varied ethnic backgrounds and faiths were all most comfortable and matter-of-fact about angels. Where had all this information and wisdom come from? David Hay and Rebecca Nye conducted a three-year investigation into children's spirituality and discovered that children are capable of having profound beliefs and meaningful spiritual experiences from a very early age. What children have told me and others about angels only seems to confirm this finding. I have singled out two particular groups of children in my acknowledgements for their profundity. Many of their pearls of wisdom can be found scattered throughout this book.

Are we born with a spiritual blueprint – DNA of the divine, passed on intact through the ages only to be suppressed from our consciousness as we grow? It has been revealed that symbols, signs and myths are more powerful if they have been meaningful in one form or another through the ages. Angels have been recorded and illustrated for thousands of years. They have always been perceived as beings who visit us to reassure, rescue or comfort. There has been traditionally a close relationship between children and angels of all religions. I trust the stories in this book will help you to look again at angels through the eyes of a child.

Acknowledgements

I am indebted to my friend and colleague David Lomax for his considerable help and support with research, and for giving his advice and precious time. To my editor Judith Kendra, a huge thank you for her understanding and encouragement. To Emma Heathcote, thanks for her considerable practical help and generosity; also to the staff at New Church College for their tolerance. Finally a big thank you to my family, Ross and Gillian, who have to live with me during the process of writing books. In particular a special thank you to my daughter Rachel for her practical help and patience.

Without my contributors there would not be a book of course and I cannot thank enough these special people. Firstly the children and staff of Walverden County Primary School, Nelson; also the children and staff of Stand Unitarian Sunday School, Manchester. Last, but by no means least, the people who gave me their very personal stories. Thank you to: Diane Balshaw, Nancy Bennet, Janice Brace, Victoria Bradley, Maggy Brook, Enid Case, Margaret Cook, Helen Coyle, Judith

Cosgrove, Carol Cox, Laura Deakin, Bella Forman, James Giles, Gillian Gordon, Lesley Gorton, Josh Green, Ray Grindall, Jean Hess, Liam Humphreys, Diane Infanti, Natasha Law, Wendy Lawday, Ian Lennox Martin, Thomas Lloyd, Sue Lucas, Mary McKee, Molly Mallory, Daniel Martin, Lisa Masters, Pam Moffat, Susan Moss, Fozia Mohammad, Nizamuddin, Karen Parsons, Jean Peart, Melody Poole, Valerie Porter, Suzanne Price, Catherine Scott, Lucy Sheldrake, Rebecca Shepherd, Judith Shrimpton JP, Paul Spence, Jean Stilwell, Jenny Tozier, Glenys Veal, Yvonne and Louise Waddington, Irene Wheeldon, Maeve Whitfield, Joyce and Paul Wiggins, Jane Wilde. I must also thank Anna, Rita, Amanda, Nick, Pamela and Holly.

Babies and Angels

It is a common belief that babies have a profound connection with angels, and an innate ability to 'see' at a spiritual level. This ability gradually decreases as the child grows, until by adulthood few of us retain the spiritual connection. Gaining knowledge in other spheres apparently bolts the door on the spiritual world.

In researching this book, I have lost count of the number of people who told me they were convinced that babies had the ability to see angels. They had seen an infant stare at a spot in the room, often the ceiling, and break into the most wonderful smile or chuckle, delighted by some form of unseen communication. Often a baby would lift its arms towards this source as if wanting to be lifted. Adults could find no explanation for this and certainly could see nothing themselves.

Since the beginning of time, across all cultures and all religions, from the frozen wastes to the desert heat, there have been accounts of angels and their contact with children. The stories in this book span the globe, cover every family and social background. I feel they are quite remarkable, but read on and judge for your-self.

One very old lady wrote to me telling me of the heartbreak her whole family suffered when her great-granddaughter died at only a few months old. Seconds before she died this very sick baby suddenly opened her eyes, beamed at a spot on the ceiling and stretched out her arms. The grieving family concluded that an angel must have appeared to the baby to take her to heaven. It was the only consolation they had on that distressing day.

In many rescue stories that involve babies and very tiny children, angelic intervention seems to be the only explanation. Two dramatic stories were reported in the press during the summer of 1998 which left everyone involved quite astonished.

Firstly you may recall the sad occasion in the UK when a grandfather, taking his small grandson on a ride in the English countryside, plunged down the side of a mountain after apparently losing control of the car. Tragically the grandfather was thrown from the car and killed, leaving his thirteen-month-old grandson alone for three days and nights. The newspapers reported that the little boy was protected from the hot sun by day and the rain and cold at night by being hidden in thick bracken. Eventually a young boy found him in amazingly good health considering his ordeal. Everyone talked of miracles, including the coroner involved in the case. I was most impressed, however, by the words of the senior police officer conducting the investigation. He said, 'Something or somebody not of this world was looking after that little boy.' Many people commented that it must have been his guardian angel.

The second incident occurred in France when a young English couple on holiday watched in horror as their car plunged down a ravine with their baby still strapped into his car seat. Believing they must certainly have lost their baby, they scrambled down the steep slope to where the vehicle had finally come to rest. Astonishingly, the baby was unhurt. He was still sitting safely in his car seat. Again the headlines talked of miracles and guardian angels.

Rescue stories, almost identical in nature, have reached me from all corners of the world. They include accounts of babies in runaway prams and toddlers wandering into danger only to emerge unscathed, rescued by unseen hands. Gill's is very typical of these stories. Pushing her new-born baby to the shops one spring morning along an extremely busy road, Gill reached the window of the local estate agents. Desperate to find another house away from the non-stop heavy traffic, she paused to look into the window. The pram was as new as the baby, and perhaps the brake needed firmer pressure than Gill had applied, for suddenly it rolled swiftly towards the busy road. Gill turned in time to see the pram with its precious occupant roll into the centre of the road. Dashing forward, she caught the pram and, heart beating, returned with it to safety. It was only moments later when she had calmed down that she realised that, for the first time anyone could remember, the road had been totally clear of traffic for those few moments. Normally, huge lorries were thundering past; heavy traffic was non-stop from early morning until late at night. Gill could scarcely comprehend the complete lack of traffic at the precise moment her baby was in such danger, but believed the baby's guardian angel must have intervened.

Another young mother faced with an identical accident saw with relief a man rush into the road to rescue her child in its pram. When the pram was returned to her, she exclaimed, 'Thank God!' The man replied, 'Yes, indeed,' and then he disappeared.

Mavis has few doubts about babies' ability to commune with angels, after the story of her granddaughter's christening. The day was bound to be filled with joy and sadness, since Robert, Mavis's husband, had died only days after Faith had been born. It was a perfect spring day. Daffodils and blossom filled the church grounds; new life in all its forms met the happy family. Mavis entered the elegant old church filled with the thought that Robert would have loved to be there with them.

Quietness fell on the family group as the service started. A spiritual atmosphere encompassed the congregation, including Faith, who gazed intently into the minister's eyes. At six months old Faith was usually extremely lively and wriggled constantly, so it was a surprise to everyone, especially her mother, to see her so calm and intent on the proceedings. The water was poured over Faith's head, and still she did not murmur.

As the service was drawing to a close, the minister held Faith whilst speaking some closing words. The family stood in a semicircle surrounding the font – parents, godparents, grandparents, and finally on the very edge of the semicircle, Mavis. Slowly and quite systematically, Faith gazed around the gathering. She stared intently at each face in turn. Her gaze met

Mavis's. Mavis found herself thinking, 'Robert, I know she would have loved you so much.' Faith's gaze moved on to the empty space at the side of Mavis, her face broke into a huge smile, and at the same moment Mavis felt the sensation of an arm around her waist. Robert is here after all on a visit from the angelic realms, she thought.

Miraculous Rescues

At certain times in our lives we all feel in need of rescue. Childhood can be a particularly hazardous time. Oblivious to the probable consequences, a child will climb the highest rock on the seashore, dive into rivers on hot days, and ride a bike like a demon through the heaviest of traffic. Parents cannot always be two steps behind, waiting in case an accident looks likely. Some children are, it seems, fortunate enough to receive extra help and protection.

For a very short period in my early teens I was the owner of a bicycle. The co-ordination required to ride the machine successfully largely eluded me. I had little skill and even less road sense, and after a few months my cycling days were over. Freewheeling down a very steep hill, I came into contact with a raised iron cover. The resulting somersault convinced me forever that bicycles and I were never intended to mix.

Jean recalls a truly remarkable rescue, one which amazed me when I heard it. At fifteen years of age she was an excellent cyclist, travelling almost everywhere by bike. She was confident, skilful and felt very safe. One busy stretch of road near her home was particularly familiar. Jean regularly used this route and knew every metre thoroughly. There was a large factory along this road where heavy lorries rumbled in and out of the gates at all times. She was always extra vigilant when approaching these gates.

One day Jean cycled along this familiar route to visit a friend for lunch. A fellow cyclist overtook her, and reached the entrance of the gates just ahead of her. Turning his head, he shouted over his shoulder to Jean that all was clear for her to proceed, and signalled to her to keep pedalling.

Suddenly, a single-decker bus hit Jean's bicycle side on with a huge impact. The chances of Jean surviving such an impact were very slim. To her astonishment, however, she felt herself lifted from the bike a fraction of a second before the impact. Unseen hands carried her some six metres from the scene ahead of the bus, and deposited her gently on the grass verge by the roadside next to a hawthorn bush.

Reality was suspended as she tried to come to terms with what had happened. Gazing up at the hawthorn bush and then at her bike, which was now a crushed lump of metal, she could only stare in utter bewilderment. She explained that the feeling she had experienced was like being lifted into the air by an invisible giant. Today, Jean is convinced that those invisible arms belonged to her guardian angel, who carried her

swiftly out of danger. She is forever grateful and certain that whatsoever befalls her, she is never alone.

Miracles take place every day of the week in
hospitals. A patient receives a new kidney or
heart, a hip joint is replaced, or a baby is
born. These are all miracles, especially for the people
involved. For one small girl of just four years of age a
miracle occurred which totally bewildered staff and
family alike.

Lucy was carried into St Mary's Hospital at
Paddington in London on a stretcher and in a very dangerous condition. Following the stretcher was a small
procession of people, including her distraught parents
accompanied by a grey-faced policeman and a third
man, anxious and agitated. It was clear some dramatic
event had occurred.

Two medical students in the casualty department
braced themselves of the worst. As third-year students
they were not new to emergencies, but the sight of this
small girl tugged at their heart strings. The policeman
told them what had happened. Lucy had run on
impulse into the middle of the extremely busy
Edgware Road, before anyone's reactions were quick
enough to prevent her. With a sickening thud a large

lorry had run over the small girl, the wheels going completely over the small body not once but twice, as the rear wheels also could not avoid Lucy.

Judith and Jenny were practical and professional medical students, and at the end of a thorough examination they were surprised to find that apart from one small bruise on her shoulder Lucy appeared to be unmarked. All exchanged confused glances. How could this be possible? The next stage would have to be X-rays and the doctor was just about to organise this procedure when to everyone's astonishment Lucy opened her eyes. She smiled broadly at everyone and asked, 'Where is the man in white?' The doctor stepped forward. 'I am here,' he said. 'No, no,' she replied, 'I mean the man in the long white shiny dress.' Judith held her hand and stroked her face. 'The man did that,' Lucy said to the startled crowd. 'He stroked my face as he picked me up, and the lorry wheels did not touch me.'

At this point Lucy fell into a completely normal sleep. Over the next twenty-four hours full medical examinations took place, but revealed nothing untoward. Only the small bruise on the shoulder gave evidence of anything at all having happened.

To say everyone involved was baffled would be an understatement. The lorry driver was still insisting he felt two distinct bumps. The policeman and the witness still insist they saw it all clearly. Lucy herself never wavered in her account of the man in white who held the lorry off her small frame. Medical staff could offer no logical explanation. Judith explained that as a medical student, angels were normally out of her field of expertise. She still tells the story, however, and adds that miracles certainly do happen in hospitals.

Extensive research has taught me that angels appear in all shapes and sizes. People seem to see what they can cope with, particularly children. Whilst a gentle light or sweet smell are enough to comfort some, others cope extremely well with a more dramatic sight. It is often when someone is in great danger that a more dramatic figure of an angel will appear. Children often encounter tiny angels or see children who have gone on before them to heaven.

Occasionally I have been told about a series of events which are far from the normal pattern, and which one would assume would frighten a child. Not so in the case of Victoria, who calmly coped with the most dramatic sighting I have ever heard of. Victoria was five years old when these remarkable events took place in Sussex, England. Like most children she fiercely resisted bedtime. It was rapidly becoming a nightly battle to get her in bed and asleep. Her mother became increasingly weary of this constant battle, trying every tactic she knew to try and settle the little girl.

On this particular occasion Victoria's mother was desperate. Weary and at her wits' end, she resigned herself to the situation and limply asked, 'Please go to sleep.' She walked downstairs quite at a loss as to what to do next to resolve the situation. Victoria flew into a tantrum, which eventually blew itself out when she realised that her mother was not responding. She was beginning to realise that her mother could not take much more that day.

Still full of mischief however, Victoria slipped out of bed and crept to the bedroom doorway, shouting defiantly 'I am coming downstairs.' There was no reply. Her mother hoped if she simply ignored her she would go back to bed. At this moment Victoria was literally struck dumb by an awesome sight. There in the doorway blocking her way was a huge African warrior! He was immensely tall, even by a little girl's standards, and carried a spear. He was dressed in the traditional grass skirt. Yet Victoria felt no fear at all, just a sense of peace and love, which washed over her until she was filled with a great desire to snuggle up in bed and sleep. Climbing into bed she smiled at the figure, closed her eyes and fell into a deep sleep.

For years Victoria kept this a secret, thinking no-one would ever believe her. When she told her mother, she suggested that it was perhaps her mother's guardian angel sent to give her a little peace and respite from her daughter. Her mother answered, however, that she was fairly certain that it was Victoria's own guardian angel protecting her from a nasty fall. Had Victoria continued on her determined route along a small corridor and down the stairs, there was a good chance that she might have fallen – and immediately at the bottom of the stairs was a large glass door, lethal to anyone falling against it.

Angels may appear in all shapes and sizes and indeed in different forms, as we have seen, but for some children a voice is all they need to keep them from harm.

Fairgrounds had never been Amanda's idea of fun, but she realised that for her sons they were the nearest thing to heaven. After a great deal of pleading, she eventually promised a trip to the fair. The evening was far from ideal. A persistent drizzle filled the air, making everywhere misty and unpleasantly damp. As she backed the car down the drive, Amanda thought with relief that at least they had not far to go. A few minutes' drive would be sufficient to reach the field, where the fair was in full swing. Adam, aged four, and Ben, only six, chatted excitedly as they set out.

Initially the road was narrow, but soon it opened out to reveal fields on either side and a clear view of the main road ahead. Switching on the windscreen wipers and polishing the inside of the window to afford a better view, she was startled when Ben suddenly shouted, 'Stop, Mummy, now!' There was such urgency in his voice that Amanda did an automatic emergency stop. It flashed through her mind that perhaps Ben was feeling ill or in pain.

Seconds later, however, they were hit by another car, which had inexplicably crossed the road to their side and hit the driver's door full on. The impact pushed Amanda's car into the field where it came to a juddering halt. Fortunately, little damage had occurred and all were uninjured. It was revealed that the oncoming driver had skidded on a patch of oil. He was also unhurt and relieved to see that the occupants of their car were in good shape. He remarked that had they been moving at the time of impact, the collision would have been so much worse.

They returned home and told their father of the event. Sipping a hot drink and glad to be in one piece, Amanda asked Ben why he had shouted. Had he seen the oncoming car skid? Was that why he had shouted as loudly as he did? 'No,' said Ben, 'the voice told me.' Everyone fell silent until Ben's father said, 'I do believe you have a guardian angel.'

It was hot, even for Arizona. The pool was the only place to feel comfortable, and Gloria was grateful for her air-conditioned home. It was therefore a fairly easy decision when her daughter Jody's birthday was

approaching for her parents to plump for a pool party –
outdoor fun, and lots of space for the children to let off
steam. Jody and her two brothers were very excited at
the prospect, and eagerly became involved in the
preparations.

The birthday arrived, and soon the garden was full
of excited children, splashing and laughing in the hot
sun. Most children living in that environment can
swim as naturally as they walk, but Carolyn was a
notable exception. No-one understood why, but she
was afraid of the water. To her mother's knowledge
there had never been a frightening incident that could
have provoked such fear, but the fact remained that she
was very reluctant to go anywhere near water, and certainly would not join the other children in the pool.
However, she enjoyed herself, and joined in everything
except the swimming competition.

Feeling that the heat and all the cheering was giving
her a sore throat, Carolyn walked to the far side of the
pool to help herself to a soft drink. Eagerly running
back around the poolside in order not to miss any of
the fun, she suddenly caught her foot on a chair, and
before she knew it she was in the water and sinking. It
was her worst nightmare come true. Incredibly, no-
one witnessed this, nor even heard her through the
laughter, especially as they all had their backs to
the pool, engrossed in a game. Feeling the bottom of
the pool beneath her, Carolyn thrashed in blind panic.

Only seconds later, she became aware of arms

holding her, strongly gripping her from behind and lifting her to the surface. A clear memory of rising from the water and being placed gently on the poolside remains with her. At last she cried out and sobbed loudly, attracting attention. A surge of people dashed to her aid.

Carolyn's mother was quite distraught, and when the commotion had subsided thought it best that they should go home. Recapping what had happened slowly and step-by-step, she talked Carolyn through the incident. Finally Carolyn said she had not even seen who had lifted her from the pool, she was so upset. Her mother stared at her daughter in disbelief, having turned and witnessed her crying on the side of the pool. She concluded that she had merely slipped in from the steps and had climbed out herself. There was no-one on the far side of the pool, and no-one could have reached the other side quickly enough without other people seeing them.

Carolyn still insisted that she had been lifted by very strong hands from the water. 'Did you see no-one at all?' her mother asked. 'No-one,' she replied. 'In that case,' said her mother, 'we can only thank God for sending one of his angels.'

S ue and her husband were so exhausted from sleepless nights that they decided to take their child Rebecca into their own bed. The bliss was instantaneous, and all three fell into a deep sleep.

Morning came all too soon. Sue's husband climbed out of bed with a huge effort, and prepared to go to work. They lived in an old, but very pleasant flat, over-looking the sea in Brighton on the south coast of England, a bracing and scenic place to bring up a baby. From deep within the covers Sue heard her husband dashing off to work, but still extremely tired she dozed on, drifting in and out of sleep for some time. A voice penetrated her dreamy state. On waking, Sue thought that she had been dreaming or that her imagination had run away with her. Not so! The voice was there again, clear, loud, and the most beautiful voice she could ever recall hearing. The message, however, was stark: 'Your baby is going down the garden path.' Fully awake by now, Sue realised with a jolt that the bed was empty — no sign of Rebecca. Rushing to the bedroom window, she saw to her horror Rebecca shuffling at great speed towards the road.

With the speed of light, Sue dashed down the path and caught her daughter. Hugging her tightly, she then pondered on what had happened. On close inspection she deduced that the old front door had not closed properly. In his hurry to get to work on time her hus-band had not been aware of this. Yet what was she to make of the voice, and where had it come from? There was no-one in the bedroom or anywhere else in the flat, so it was improbable that the voice had come from outside. The most remarkable thing of all was the nature and tone of the voice. It was the most beautiful Sue had ever heard, and the quality was decidedly unearthly. Sue is in little doubt that her daughter was saved by an angel that morning.

Angels sit on stars wearing their sandals, because the stars are spiky and would hurt their feet.

GILLIAN, 4

Ever since she could remember, stars had fascinated Sarah. She would implore her mother to leave her bedroom curtains open, so that she could fall asleep with the stars twinkling down at her. Living in the country, with no major cities for miles, made the night sky spectacular.

One night, just before Christmas, Sarah stared at the night sky through her large bedroom window. The night was cold and clear, and the velvet sky was full of stars. With her imagination fired, she decided to get out of bed in order to get a closer look and to decide which route Santa's sleigh would take. Shivering a little, she climbed onto the rather high window sill. Full of mounting excitement at the thought of Christmas Eve, she gave a little jump for joy, and found herself catapulting backwards from the window sill, yelling as she fell towards the hard floor. She did not, however, come into contact with the floor, but instead was conscious of a floating sensation and gentle arms placing her into bed. She recalls that the bed was several feet from the window, too far for her to have simply fallen back into it. No-one was in the room and it was several seconds later that the bedroom door opened and her mother appeared to find out what the matter was.

Switching on the light, she came and sat on her daughter's bed. 'Did you have a bad dream?' she asked. Sarah told her what had happened, but her mother would not believe it was real. 'Simply a dream, darling' was all she said. Sarah knew even at that young age that it was definitely not a dream. She went to sleep, but on waking the next morning noticed that the toys that normally sat on the window sill were scattered on the floor – proof at least that she had stood on the window sill, and dislodged them in her fall.

Twenty years later the events of that night are as clear as if they had happened recently, and no-one will ever convince Sarah that she was not rescued by angel arms that night long ago.

Nick was a toddler of three when his parents took him to a fantastic fair. Eyes like saucers, he tried to take in all the wonderful sights and sounds, longing to dash in all directions at once with the sheer excitement of it all. Despite his insistent tugging for freedom, Nick's mother held firmly onto his hand. The crowds were dense, and a toddler would be lost in seconds.

A magnificent traction engine rolled past, its sheer size commanding awe. Following the monstrous engine, there was to be a display of talent in handling a coach and horses. It was a magnificent sight, the coach polished to perfection, as the hooves of the horses thundered down the display field. Nick was entranced at the sight and sounds of the horses. Without warning and with one great tug, he broke free from his mother's grip and dashed onto the field, and directly into the path of the oncoming coach and horses.

The crowd yelled, and Nick's mother screamed. It was obvious that no-one could reach him before the coach bore down. It knocked the little boy off his feet, and although the horses' hooves missed his body, the heavy coach wheels rolled right over his tiny frame.

Silence fell on the crowd. Nobody moved or seemed to know what to do next. Only Nick's parents dashed forward. To this day no-one can fully explain why, or indeed how, Nick was able to survive unharmed. In fact he was still as full of beans as ever only minutes before the event. How could this possibly be? How on earth could a huge carriage wheel roll right over the little boy and there be no evidence of it having happened? Nick, his parents, and all those who witnessed this extraordinary scene are completely at a loss as to what possible explanation there might be.

They do ask themselves from time to time: 'Did the angels rescue Nick?' You will have to decide for yourselves.

Some people are clearly close to the spiritual world from birth – or in Helen's case even before it. Helen's mother was waiting anxiously for her birth, with just three weeks to go. Sleep at this point in time was not an easy state to achieve, and on this particular night it seemed impossible. A previous baby had been born with a mental handicap, and although much loved, she hoped this baby would be perfectly normal in every way.

At last she managed to doze, only to awake suddenly with a jolt for no apparent reason. There then appeared to her, sitting at the foot of the bed, a tall figure of a man dressed in a long white robe. He had shoulder-length brown hair, and his piercing blue eyes radiated pure love and compassion. An index finger was raised to his lips as if to warn her not to shout in surprise. In a voice no louder than a whisper, he told her that the baby would be perfect. He then faded away slowly, leaving Helen's mother full of wonder, but perfectly at ease. Subsequently Helen was indeed born perfect.

Helen loved to hear her mother tell the story of that

night. She felt as if there would always be a guardian angel there for her, and a strong sense of protection stayed with her throughout childhood. Many small incidents seemed to bear this out as she grew.

In her teens Helen began to enjoy greatly outdoor sports. Growing up in Australia was a great bonus for someone who loved being outside. It was therefore a real hardship to stay indoors at the age of sixteen and study for her school exams. Helen was keen to perform well even so, and wished the whole family to be proud of her. It became a great source of worry to her, and as the exams drew close she found herself in a state of high anxiety.

One night a short time before the exams were due to start, Helen lay in bed feeling quite drained. A faint glow began to appear in the room, spreading until it was above her bed. In the centre of this glow a sensitive and beautiful face appeared. At once Helen felt calm and comforted and fell into a deep refreshing sleep. To her amazement and delight, this angel face appeared every night until the exams were completed. Helen passed the exams with flying colours, without the slightest worry, but the angel face never appeared again.

Life continued as normal, but there often seemed to be an unseen presence warning Helen; sometimes it was only a feeling or a slight sensation of a hand stopping her in her tracks. One dramatic incident took place when Helen was about to climb on board a chair lift. The lift was of the type which swung around in a continuous loop without stopping and one had to jump on as it swung behind you, so you had to be nimble.

Helen waited for her turn to climb on the chair, but it arrived so swiftly she scarcely had time to sit in it securely before she was whisked away. Climbing sharply and with speed, Helen struggled to gain a secure seat-hold, but slid off the edge. Plunging to the ground in terror, she felt sure some terrible injuries would ensue, as did the horrified crowd of bystanders who screamed involuntarily. Immediately before coming into contact with the ground, from several metres high, she had the sensation of hands catching her. Gaining consciousness was her next memory. She had fainted with shock, but did not have a single scratch as a result of the fall.

The final story of Helen's continuing protection took place one hot sunny day when a crowd of friends headed for the beach. Heading for Oberon Bay in Wilson's Promontory National Park, they walked down the path to the shore amongst beautiful scenery. A feeling of being held back suddenly overcame Helen, and she stopped dead in her tracks in time to see a poisonous snake slide across their path. Silently saying thank you, she continued to the beach. This was Helen's favourite place and swimming was her favourite outdoor sport. She was usually the first into the water and the last to come out.

The crowd of young people raced to the water, and

several of Helen's friends swiftly swam past her going further out into the bay. They yelled at Helen to follow them, and were slightly puzzled when she hesitated, as it was completely out of character. Normally there would not have been a moment's hesitation. Again Helen was feeling that some force, unseen and unheard, was preventing her from going any further. Turning she swam back to the beach and joined some of her less adventurous colleagues.

No more than ten minutes had elapsed, when to everyone's horror a huge freak wave sent Helen's friends in the water crashing onto the outlying rocks. Scrambling to try and secure a hold, they were unaware that a second large wave was descending on them. People on the shore watched helplessly as one of the friends was swept away by the force of the wave. It was more than twenty-four hours before his body was found. A happy end-of-term picnic had turned into a tragedy. However, for Helen, it seemed once more that she had been warned and protected.

One glorious autumn day Lucy decided to go for a long ride on her pony Clover. The pony had been a thirteenth birthday present for Lucy, and she loved him dearly. Since she lived in a fairly quiet open part of the country, she started her ride trotting down the leafy lanes behind her home, enjoying the crunchy sounds of the fallen leaves under Clover's hooves. Presently they came to a fork in the road where Lucy would usually turn right, which would take her on a long circular route back to the starting point. Today, however, she was feeling a great deal more adventurous, and decided Clover was ready for a much longer ride. They would have to cross a rather busy road at this point, but Clover was used to traffic, and it would only be a very short stretch of road before they could turn into the quiet lanes once more.

Turning to the left, they heard the buzz of traffic, and slowed to a walk as they approached the road. Clover behaved impeccably, halting on command at the busy road. Calmly crossing the road when a break in the traffic allowed, they walked along the far side of the road until they could reach the turning point to leave the busy traffic behind. Passing under a railway bridge should be no problem and they would be there. But trotting under the bridge both Lucy and Clover were startled by being overtaken by a very fast and noisy car. The fact that they were in a short tunnel must have amplified the noise, and Clover was very scared. Panicking, the pony reared, and threw Lucy into the road where she landed heavily.

Traffic screeched to a standstill, a mobile phone was used to call an ambulance immediately, and in record time help arrived. The ambulance personnel were examining Lucy before taking her to hospital. Lucy, however, was astonished to find that she was watching this scene from the underside of the bridge. She was looking down on her own body lying in the road, and could see and hear the ambulance men making their checks. A woman had taken hold of Clover and was calming him, but Lucy was apparently floating above it all. She was aware of a warm light surrounding her and the sensation that it was supporting her. A voice then spoke to her gently and told her not to be afraid.

Her next memory is one of cold and pain washing over her as she was lifted onto a stretcher. She realised that she was back in her body and on the way to hospital. There were no serious injuries, and recovery was fairly swift. Soon she was home, and then had time to reflect on the incident. Her parents pondered on what it could mean and what the voice could have been. Lucy, however, has no reservations. She states categorically that she was cared for by an angel.

It has often been said that we are all psychically gifted, but untutored and underdeveloped in the art. It does seem to be a phenomenon which comes more easily to some people than others, though from time to time we all have premonitions. For certain people the warning or premonition is so powerful there is no mistaking the message. Valerie is one of those people. She will often get not only a feeling that something may be wrong, but also a clear voice in her head telling her what action to take. Valerie firmly believes this is her guardian angel, and can recall six or seven times since childhood when the voice has spoken to her. On several occasions she has been led to situations where as a trained nurse she feels she was needed at that particular time.

The last time Valerie heard this voice it was especially welcome, as it involved the safety of her twelve-year-old son David. She had left him playing with a group of boys happily if noisily in their neighbour's garden to visit the local supermarket. The neighbour had built his own sons an excellent treehouse.

Ten minutes later Valerie was parking her car at the supermarket. Sighing, she switched off the engine, and collected her thoughts along with the shopping list. Turning to open the car door she was shaken by the insistence and clarity of the voice speaking to her. 'Go home at once,' it said, twice. Quickly fastening her seatbelt, Valerie set off for home as fast as the traffic and the speedlimit would allow. Dashing down the path to her neighbour's garden, she saw her son on the ground, surrounded by white-faced children and very concerned adults. David had fallen from the treehouse, landing heavily, and it was apparent to Valerie that he had broken his leg. An ambulance was on its way but

Valerie took over in a professional mode that curtailed the rising panic of her parent role.

Days later, when the confusion had died down and David was in plaster, her friend next door asked 'By the way, what made you come dashing home so quickly from the supermarket that day?' 'A message from on high,' was Valerie's enigmatic answer.

Glenys and her parents were planning a trip to the seaside, and the excitement was intense for the little girl. A picnic was planned, and so sandwiches and a flask were placed in the car and they set off in high spirits.

Approximately half way to their intended destination, Glenys was watching the sky for any sign of rain that might spoil the day. She then saw the most fascinating formation. Against the blue sky a huge cloud had formed into a giant figure. Glenys decided that this must be Jesus. Leaning forward she tapped her mother on the shoulder and said, 'We must not worry, everything will be all right. Jesus is watching over us.' Her mother was startled, to put it mildly, but she smiled at the little girl and said 'Yes dear, of course, thank you.'

Only a few moments after this conversation, the car hit an object close to the curb and Glenys's father lost control. Over and over the car rolled, before landing on its side several hundred metres away. No-one could believe that all three members of the family were completely unhurt, escaping without a scratch. Glenys, however, was not in the least bit surprised.

I am sure we all recall getting into scrapes as children because we disobeyed parental instruction. Kind people rescue some of us, whilst others flounder alone as best they can. For some children, however, it seems very special help is at hand. Margaret can recall several occasions throughout her life when she feels extra special help was at hand, and so she feels truly blessed.

At the age of eight, Margaret was allocated to take her little sister for a walk in the pushchair. She was joined by her good friend Peter. Margaret was more than old enough to understand the rules when going out unaccompanied by an adult, but she was especially warned on their departure not to go anywhere near the canal. This was completely out-of-bounds and to be avoid in all circumstances.

Curiosity is never far away in childhood, and inevitably they found themselves at the canal. There were numerous nooks and crannies to be explored, and Margaret and Peter decided to climb up the steep sides of the bank. They left her sister in her pushchair, and told her to stay put and sit still while they scrambled up the bank. She sat still for less than a minute, and pulling the pushchair after her, tried to follow the other two children up the steep bank. The inevitable happened, and she let go of the chair which immediately ran down the steep slope and straight into the canal. Margaret heard the loud splash and was gripped with fear. Not only was the expensive pushchair in the canal, but it was festooned with coats and hats. Panic and guilt rose in Margaret in equal measures at the thought of her mother's reaction. She had disobeyed a strict instruction, and it was a miracle that her little sister had not fallen into the canal also.

Margaret burst into tears, and found herself praying. What she expected to happen she did not quite know, but it was the only thing she could think of under the circumstances. It seemed that an answer to her prayers appeared in the form of a tall boy carrying a long carved pole. In a trice he had retrieved the pushchair from the water, complete with belongings.

The boy disappeared as quickly as he had come, and Margaret could only stand and stare with amazement. She reflected later that it was far too much of a coincidence that a boy with exactly the right implement to help had arrived at the precise time he was needed. He had a rather special air about him, and was certainly a little mysterious. She concluded that he must have been an angel in disguise.

The protection continued for Margaret as she grew. She was once saved by millimetres from a speeding car completely out of control. Walking down her garden path one day, a huge ridge tile fell and missed her head by a fraction. These and similar incidents have followed Margaret all her life, but the most dramatic incident happened on holiday fairly recently in Keflonica, Greece. Travelling with friends in a car along a very twisty and winding road through the hills, she was only too aware of the sheer drop on each side of the road and the fact that there was not a single barrier to help prevent accidents. The day was wet and misty and the drive distinctly hazardous.

Everyone's worst nightmare was realised when the car skidded on the wet road, and spinning out of control went backwards at speed over the edge and down the steep slope, which was almost a sheer drop. The car thundered through dense foliage until eventually it hit an olive tree. Lurching violently it came to rest on its side in the tree. Rescuers were quickly on the scene, and were surprised and relieved to find all the occupants of the car shaken but completely unhurt.

On reaching the top of the gorge again, Margaret and her friends reflected on just how fortunate they had been. Miraculously they had missed by only a metre or so a giant rock protruding from the hillside. The olive tree was the only tree on that slope, yet it had caught them and effectively prevented them from hurtling down the sheer drop to certain death at the bottom of the valley.

Little wonder that Margaret believes her guardian angel is watching over her still.

'Please, Mum, can I have rollerblades for Christmas?' Mary groaned. Three times in one week she had heard Liam's plaintive cry, and it was only October. She was very worried at the prospect of rollerblades. The local park had provided an area where the youngsters could rollerblade, but to reach it a very busy main road had to be crossed, and Mary had often seen boys dicing with death crossing this road with their rollerblades on their feet.

Inevitably the parents succumbed, and on Christmas morning Liam found his much desired rollerblades under the Christmas tree. He was beside himself with excitement and could scarcely wait to be off to test them. However, he had to promise faithfully not to cross the busy road wearing the blades, but to put them on when he arrived at the park. He promised, of course, and for the next few days the blades scarcely left his feet. Mary watched him go, uttering a silent prayer for his safe keeping.

Soon Liam had become extremely proficient on his

rollerblades, and was capable of performing all kinds of skilful manoeuvres. He began to believe he was almost invincible and was as safe wearing blades as he was on two feet. One evening as dusk was falling, Liam set off for home, leaving the park with his friends. He reasoned that surely by now he did not need to keep removing his blades before crossing the road; he was after all something of an expert at this point, confident and in control. Waving to his friends and glancing only perfunctorily in both directions, he launched himself into the momentarily clear road.

To this day Liam has no idea where the car came from, he only recalls a large red vehicle bearing down on him at great speed. The car struck him virtually head on, but instead of the full impact one would have expected, it felt like a glancing blow, and Liam found himself being lifted high enough for the car to pass underneath his body. He soared through the air in an arc-like movement, and found himself being lowered gently onto his feet. He was safe and sound on the opposite pavement, shocked but in one piece.

A family friend who witnessed the accident told Liam's mother it had been like watching a film with special effects. The boy appeared to float across the road high in the air with no visible means of support. Liam insists that he had a definite sensation of hands holding him until he was out of harm's way. Mary concludes that her prayer had been heard and indeed answered by his guardian angel.

Heaven Scent

I always think that certain smells and fragrances are
as powerfully evocative as music or photographs.
They whisk us back to childhood, or provoke
memories of a certain person in our lives. I am sure
each one of us has experienced such sensory triggers.
In recent years when people have been a good deal
more forthcoming about angelic encounters and experiences, I hear more and more stories involving a fragrance with an angelic source. It appears that the
beautiful aroma people experience at time of trouble
or when comfort was needed had never previously
been connected to a heavenly intervention. When
stories began to emerge, it was obvious that at last people had an explanation for their own personal, inex-
plicable fragrance. For example, one woman who
could frequently smell her husband's tobacco smoke,
years after his death, was delighted to read another
similar story. At last she realised it was not her imagination but as she had always hoped – her husband
assuring her whenever she felt particularly low that he
was never far away.

J ane will never forget the fragrance that changed
her life, but she struggles to identify it. If you have
ever been marooned in a caravan with rain relent-
lessly beating on the roof, you will know how depressing it can be. Add to this mixture two frustrated small
children, and you will begin to understand how Jane
was feeling. The idea of a caravan holiday had sounded
most attractive, however, when her friend said she
thought a break would be beneficial. It was a beautiful
area and the caravan was comfortable and tastefully
furnished, but no sooner had they arrived and settled
in, than it began to rain. The heavy downpour turned
to torrential rain, and two whole days passed with very
little respite.

Miraculously the third day dawned dry with fairly
clear skies. Like greased lightning, they dashed from
the caravan and down the mountain in the car to the
nearest seaside town. By mid-afternoon the light was
beginning to fade, so Jane thought it best that they
should return to the caravan, and then head for home
while it was still dry. Packing their things into the car,
they felt that at least they had enjoyed one fine day, and
set off in good spirits. The road was quite muddy from
all the recent rain and Jane drove with extra care.

It could not have been more than half an hour from

leaving the caravan site that the rain started again. High winds added to her problems, and the rain became so heavy that the windscreen wipers could scarcely cope. They were in the midst of a storm, and the light had gone completely. Scarcely able to see, Jane stopped the car for a moment, although what she could do about the situation she had no idea. Tears ran down her face as she looked at the two little girls on the back seat. The three-year-old was fast asleep, oblivious to their predicament, but her five-year-old daughter smiled perkily at her. This made Jane cry all the more. It was then that this wise little girl leant forwards, placed her hand on her mother's shoulders and said, 'Don't cry mummy, the angels will help us.' Smiling at the little one, she replied 'Of course, dear.' Drying her eyes on a tissue, she started the car again and was prepared to struggle on. The rain did seem less heavy now, and within minutes it had stopped completely.

Astonishment gripped Jane when suddenly the car was filled with the most powerful aroma. It was almost impossible to identify, like no other smell she had ever encountered. Perfume, flowers and spices all mixed together was the nearest she could come to a description, and it filled her with hope and confidence. The fragrance engulfed them completely for about a minute before gradually fading. Jane drove on with renewed confidence and composure.

Safe in bed at home Jane relived the events of the night. She found herself thinking, 'Where on earth did that fragrance come from?' but she knew in her heart that it was not of this earth at all.

Every raindrop that falls is accompanied by an angel,
for even a raindrop is a manifestation of a being.
MOHAMMED

Death is never easy to cope with, and the loss of some-one close and much loved is the hardest thing we ever have to face emotionally. Adults find the experience daunting and emotionally draining, but what about children? How does one begin to explain, comfort and reassure a grieving child?

Rebecca was nine years old when her mother died, and people told her that her mother was now an angel in heaven. All Rebecca knew was that her mother was no longer there, and the only tangible evidence left was a wardrobe full of her clothes and personal effects. Opening the wardrobe, Rebecca could smell her mother's perfume, which made her feel close for a moment. Along with her elder sister, she resolved to be brave and pull together with their much loved father.

Months and years passed, and eventually the pain eased, though Rebecca never forgot her mother. There were moments when she felt low and missed her dreadfully. It was on one of these days that Rebecca felt slightly unwell as well as missing her mother. Late in the afternoon she lay on the sofa in the lounge, home alone for a while. Sinking back into the comfortable cushions, she relaxed and started to think about the days in the past when if she was feeling unwell her mother would pamper her for a while.

Suddenly, through the door from the hall came the most wonderful fragrance. It completely enveloped Rebecca before wafting on through the lounge. It was instantly recognisable to her; she had no doubt at all it was her mother's. Not only did it contain her perfume but also all the other fragrances and smells which composed her mother's life – the medicine she had taken when she had been ill, her shampoo and lots of other smells. She was in no doubt that this was an indication of her mother's presence, an unmistakable way of letting her daughter know that she was not alone and still loved very much.

Since that time, on several occasions and in different places, Rebecca has experienced the all-enveloping aroma, usually at times when she needs comfort or when she feels a little weary. She knows for certain that throughout her life her mother will never be far away.

Maggy suffered the loss of her mother when she was only twelve years old. Her father was a devout Christian, and had decided that

SAINT GREGORIOS, PARUMALA
(M.E. 1835-1870)
ഇടവഴയുടെ തഥാ പരിശുദ്ധനായ
പരുമല കൊച്ചുതിരുമേനി

ARTIST BABOO
UZHATHIL
CHENGANNUR
KERALA

PUBLISHED BY
M.&.M. BOOKS & PHOTO STALL
THOPPIL BUILDING
PARUMALA P.O. MANNAR.

Baboo, CHENGANNUR-CH-1987

he wanted the funeral service in the family home. The coffin was brought into the lounge for several days before the service.

After the funeral, Maggy was amazed to find the room where her mother's coffin had lain full of the perfume of spring flowers. She would frequently go into the room to experience the most wonderful scent she could ever recall.

It was only later when she was an adult that she fully realised that this was a most unusual phenomenon. True, there had been flowers at the time of her mother's funeral service and when the coffin was laid in the lounge. When flowers are removed, however, the fragrance does not last for more than a few hours. The fragrance of spring flowers in Maggy's home lasted for more than twelve months.

I have been informed over and over again recently that the perfume of yellow roses accompanies prayers answered by St Theresa. Yellow roses are apparently a calling card of the saint and feature prominently in stories of help attributed to her.

Enid Case wrote a fascinating book some twenty years ago entitled *The Odour of Sanctity*; she kindly gave me permission to retell one of her stories here.

At the age of five, Cynthia was diagnosed as having a heart murmur. The aortic valve leading from the heart was giving great cause for concern and a close watch would have to be kept on the little girl. For years she was carefully monitored, and at the age of twelve was taken into Blackpool's Victoria Hospital for surgery. This was the only course to be taken if she was to live, yet it carried a huge risk. Friends and family gathered around to pray for the little girl. Many people prayed specifically to St Theresa as the child underwent the ten hours of intensive surgery.

Arriving home, Cynthia's parents walked up the path to the front door. They were a little bewildered at a fine mist which appeared from nowhere and completely surrounded them. It was decidedly aromatic, and as they stepped into the house they were overcome by the scent of roses. There were no flowers of any description in the house. The garden had no roses in bloom, though in her confusion Cynthia's mother went outdoors to check. It was then that Cynthia's sister arrived home and asked, 'What is that wonderful smell? It followed me all down the path and into the house.'

Needless to say the operation was a huge success. In fact after only seventeen days, and to everyone's astonishment, Cynthia came home from the hospital. The entire family to this day are amazed at the events of that evening. Time after time they hear people talk about the smell of roses being an answer to prayers directed to St Theresa, and they would certainly not disagree.

Communication with angels starts if you recognise
they are there.
MURRAY STEINMAN

Irene liked the smell of her little baby boy, especially after his evening bath. She felt a very special bond with her son, so was overcome with shock and grief when he died. However in time, much to her joy, another baby arrived, another son whom she named Zac. A healthy child, he grew swiftly into a toddler. Irene could not help but wonder what her first child would have looked like at this stage; she knew they would still have been close. Pondering on this thought and remembering just how close they had been, she tucked her son Zac into his bed for the night.

A strong feeling of a presence in the room took Irene by surprise. This was accompanied by a fragrance so powerful and beautiful that words fail to describe it, she says. It had appeared quickly and it vanished with equal speed leaving her bewildered. The thought came into her mind subsequently that this was her first-born son contacting her and telling her he was near.

Zac grew up and to Irene's delight over the years on many significant occasions, the fragrance would engulf her as completely as on that first night. The day arrived when Zac was independent enough to leave home, and he decided to acquire a house of his own. It came as no surprise to Irene when Zac's girlfriend told her that on entering the house for the first time, she was amazed to find it full of the most beautiful fragrance, one she had never encountered before.

Angels are beautiful and they have a lovely smell.
<small>FAYE HILTON, 11</small>

Debbie's young son lay seriously ill in hospital, and she felt completely numb. On the way to the hospital she would have to stop at her grandmother's house to give her the news. Her grandmother, Martha, was quite frail and very old, so Debbie wondered how she would react. As she slowly told Martha the awful news, for a time the old lady simply sank back into her chair white-faced. Sitting up straight suddenly she said, 'Well Debbie, I will do the only thing I can and that is pray for Simon. The hospital I know will do their very best for him, but even they can use some help from above.' Debbie smiled and thanked her grandmother, then, declining the usual cup of tea, she quickly left for the hospital.

Hurrying down the hospital corridors she began to worry about what condition he would be in that morning. She too started to pray that her child would recover and return to them. The day wore on, and Simon's father joined Debbie at the hospital. He suggested she went home for a while, but Debbie could not bring herself to leave Simon's bedside.

Eventually a doctor arrived to check up on Simon and after examining him said he could actually detect a slight improvement. It was a ray of hope for them to cling to. Over the course of the night, Simon seemed to be slowly gaining in strength until in the early hours of the morning he opened his eyes. Parents and staff were thrilled, and in the case of the doctors more than a little surprised. 'He is a fighter,' one remarked.

By mid-morning there was a huge improvement, and the consensus was that Simon was out of danger. They still advised that he had a long way to go before a full recovery, but all the signs were now much more positive. At last Debbie broke down in tears, and the tension and grief she had blocked out of her mind flooded over her. She told her husband that she would briefly call in on Martha on the way home to give her the much more cheerful news. Martha, standing erect, answered the door. 'It's good news, Grandma,' Debbie said. 'There has been a considerable improvement in Simon's condition. We feel sure he will now make a full recovery.'

Martha smiled knowingly, 'I know,' she said, 'come in and I will explain.' It had been a long day, filled with worry and Martha had known there would be no point in her going to bed, since sleep would have been impossible. She had sat in her armchair listening to the radio for a long time, and then in the early hours she had decided to pray again. She had asked God to send his angels to help Simon, because he was so precious to them all. 'In that instant the room filled with a heady perfume, completely enveloping me and the whole room,' she said. It had faded very quickly but Martha had known her prayers had been heard. 'Could you say exactly when this was?' Debbie asked. 'I think it must have been around 2 a.m.,' she replied, 'for that was when I had switched off the radio.' Debbie thought with a great degree of certainty that it would have been around that time Simon had opened his eyes. A shiver ran through her. 'Thank you, Grandma,' she said. 'You really did help.' 'We were all touched by angels,' her grandmother replied.

It was a wet and windy Wednesday afternoon, and the sky was positively leaden, not a silver lining in sight. Celia was feeling low and wobbly after a fierce bout of influenza. Not very robust at the best of times, she knew regaining her health and strength would be a slow process. The need for fresh air at this point was, however, uppermost in her mind and she was determined to go outdoors for a little while, no matter how wet.

Pulling on her wellingtons and waterproof anorak, she set out for a short stroll to the village. Barely a soul was in sight, but somehow that suited Celia's mood, she felt even a chat would be a huge effort. It was nearly ten years since she had settled in this lovely part of the country. As an artist and illustrator of books the peace and quiet suited her well, and the beautiful scenery inspired her to work. Celia's parents had died when she was only a teenager, and she and her brother had become very close, living together for many years until the day he married and went to live abroad. Celia missed him very much but was nevertheless very happy with her life.

Finding herself at the door of the tiny bookshop in the village, she wandered inside for a browse. Aroused from her browsing by the loud, old-fashioned bell of the shop, she saw a young mother and two small boys enter. They were not local or she would have known them, and she gazed curiously as they looked around.

A large book about angels in art had taken Celia's eye, and she had it open at a particularly attractive picture. She was taken by surprise when one of the small boys sidled up to her and asked 'Is that a fairy?' Smiling she answered 'No, it's an angel,' and proceeded to tell the little boy all about angels and their functions. She realised with a jolt that he reminded her very much of how her brother had looked at that age. The youngster was clearly fascinated, and Celia told him angels were never far away.

At that instant, the old dusty bookshop was filled with the most wonderful fragrance of spring flowers, spices and dew on grass. Celia could not identify it, as it was unlike anything she had ever experienced before. The young mother looked up in surprise, and remarked that there were no flowers in sight. So where was the beautiful fragrance coming from? The door was firmly closed, and it was still drizzling. Quite a mystery it seemed.

Saying goodbye, the mother and her sons left the shop still remarking on the wonderful smell. Celia bought the book and slowly began to walk home. The little boy had indeed been introduced to angels on that wet and windy Wednesday, she thought with an inner glow. No doubt about it, she felt very much better.

Early in the hot summer of 1966, Emma was sitting under her grandmother's lilac tree, inhaling the fragrance and gazing at the beautiful blossom. Lilac had always been her favourite colour, and gazing up at the deep blue sky through the lilacs was a heady experience.

Chatting to her grandmother under the lilac tree brought them back once again to the by now more than familiar story of Emma's stay in hospital when a small child. Emma's mother, Rosemary, had told her the story many times over the years, and Florence, her grandmother, too was always ready to discuss it.

Apparently one minute Emma had been a happy, laughing child, the next dangerously ill with only a small chance of pulling through. The word 'meningitis' had hit Rosemary as hard as a brick, and she had scarcely been able to comprehend what was happening. Emma had been about four at the time, and does not recall the details, only being taken to hospital feeling very ill.

With her parents and grandmother at her bedside, and the doctors and nursing staff doing all they could to help, the night had worn on. Rosemary's husband had returned to take care of the younger child, and she and Emma's grandmother had sat by the bed during the night. The night had seemed endless, but eventually the sky had begun to lighten. Gazing through the window, tears pricking her eyes, Rosemary had found herself praying, something she had not done in a very long time: 'God send your angels to help my child.'

Turning, she had noticed that Florence was awake and looking confused. 'Where is that lovely smell coming from?' she had asked. The room had filled with the strong scent of lilac. Behind the little girl's bed a light had begun to grow, until a large ray of light fanned out over the whole room. It had lasted for about a minute or so, and then gradually had faded along with the perfume. Rosemary and Florence had stared in silence at each other. They had no idea what on earth had happened.

Shortly after this a nurse had come to check on

Emma. She had said that she was stable, and that in itself was a good sign. Telling the nurse about the incident, Rosemary had noticed a slow, knowing smile spread across her face. 'It is not the first time I have heard such a story,' the nurse had replied. 'The lilac or violet smell has been described to me on several occasions and is known as the scent of angels in the hospital.'

Hospital Angels

It seems to me that the most difficult pain to endure is that of one's children. Watching a child in pain and feeling helpless is infinitely worse than anything one might endure oneself, and it is particularly frightening when a child is taken to hospital. Friends and family will say the child is in the most appropriate place for a speedy recovery, and they are probably correct. The problem for the parent, however, is the knowledge that the child must be seriously ill to be taken to hospital in the first place.

This was certainly how Yvonne felt when she heard the awful news that her daughter had been taken to hospital. Struggling to take in the news, she was told that Louise had been taken ill, and no-one was sure what the problem was. The school had sent for an ambulance and then called her.

A brain haemorrhage was diagnosed as the problem, and Louise was very ill indeed. She lay in her hospital bed, her mother holding her hand and feeling completely helpless. Looking up, Yvonne was delighted to see two of her closest friends arriving to give support. The friends looked at the girl not sure of what to say. Not more than a minute or two elapsed when one of the friends jumped up swiftly and fled from the room. Initially taken aback, Yvonne concluded that the sight of Louise ill had upset her friend, who could not cope. It was quite understandable, and she sat with her remaining friend for some time.

To everyone's joy and relief, Louise slowly recovered until eventually she was able to return home, her usual happy self. It was only now that Yvonne discovered what had really happened that night. Whilst chatting, both of her friends had seen angels at the head of Louise's hospital bed, who had appeared in balls of light to the two girls. One friend had interpreted their presence as messengers coming to take Louise to heaven, because at any moment she would die. She had not been able to cope with this, and not realising that the other girl had also seen the angels, she had run from the room in distress. Yvonne's second friend, however, had interpreted the angels' presence completely differently, assuming that they were there to heal and comfort and that Louise would be sure to recover.

Five years have passed, and Louise is a bright, healthy girl. She believes that the angels were certainly messengers that night, and is eternally grateful that the message was in fact so positive.

B ella Forman is a very special lady from Philadelphia, USA, where she not only lectures on the subject of angels but also runs workshops and meditation groups. She very successfully helps many people and she helped one particular lady at times of great need.

Bella became a friend to this lady when she joined her meditation group. She was pregnant and had more than her share of worries ·about the pregnancy and delivery of the baby. She definitely found meditating a great help. Bella told her the angels would be only too willing to help and that she must never forget they were close. She asked Bella if her baby would have a guardian angel, and Bella replied she felt certain it would. The pregnancy continued a good deal more smoothly after this.

At last the day arrived, labour started and Bella's friend left for the hospital praying for a healthy baby. Placing her trust in the hospital staff, she went through her preparations calmly enough. This calm was not to last, for soon lots of things started to go wrong, the labour dragged on and was proving very painful and difficult. All her old fears flooded back.

Remembering Bella's words, she started to try and meditate, hoping that if she could become a little calmer it might help the situation. She also recalled Bella assuring her that the angels were ever near, and she found herself asking the angels for help. Breathing deeply, she suddenly glanced up, and to her amazement in the mirror on the wall opposite her bed she saw not one but two angels – the guardians of her and her baby. From that moment on the delivery went swiftly and smoothly, much to the surprise of the hospital staff, and to the sheer delight of the proud and grateful new mother.

J anice was just three years old when her story begins, but she is absolutely certain of the events that took place, and the memory is crystal clear to this day.

Christmas was rapidly approaching and the house was filled with all the sights and smells a child associates with this time of year. Janice stood in the kitchen watching her mother bake, and distinctly remembers starting to feel unwell. Temperature soaring, she was placed in her bed and the doctor summoned. After prescribing medicine to bring her temperature down, he left saying he would call again later because he was quite worried about her condition. Janice did not respond to the medicine and grew worse. The doctor on his return said she was seriously ill, and that if morning brought no relief or improvement they would have to admit her to hospital.

It looked like Janice might be spending Christmas in hospital, and this thought distressed her mother terribly. Morning dawned but brought little comfort, for Janice was no better, in fact she was decidedly worse. Her mother prepared herself for the certainty of having to take her daughter to hospital, and waited nervously for the doctor to arrive. Janice distinctly remembers the doctor arriving and talking to her mother downstairs. The curtains were still closed in the little bedroom and the light switched on.

Looking around the room, she saw a sight which would remain with her forever, for there looking directly at her and floating gently in the air were several small angels. She thinks that there must have been at least seven of these lovely creatures, hovering on either side of her bed. They wore long gowns of shining blue, and they definitely had wings, for she can remember the fluttering movements they produced. Most unusually, these angels were very tiny in stature – only the size of a child's doll – and appeared to be female. She even recalls their eyes, kind, intelligent and twinkly as they focused on Janice. It occurred to the little girl that they had come to take her to heaven, and when her mother returned she told her that Jesus wanted her for a sunbeam, repeating a hymn she had learned in Sunday school.

To her mother's surprise, and indeed the doctor's and all the family's, Janice looked considerably better, and in the following days made a swift and complete recovery. She told her mother about the angels' visit and her mother understood completely, never once telling the little girl she had imagined it or that she had been dreaming. Fearing that she would be laughed at, Janice kept the story a secret as she grew, but decided as an adult to tell her story in order to encourage others. She reasons that she saw such tiny beings because, as a very sick small child, an encounter with a much larger vision would have frightened her.

Angels have a map of the stars so that they can find you when you're poorly and make you better.
NICKY, 10

How often have you heard the expression 'appearances can be deceptive'? We frequently find just how off-beam our assumptions are. It happened to me with Joyce. On first meeting her, I concluded that she was a happy industrious person, socially aware, content with life, and probably had not a care in the world. Nothing could have been further from the truth. She was a contented wife and mother all right, but had come through more trauma than most of us ever have to face. At the age of thirteen her son Paul became seriously ill. The diagnosis was every parent's nightmare: malignant cancer. They were warned that the prognosis was not favourable and to be prepared for the worst possible outcome.

In a state of emotional turmoil, Joyce was sent home to try and get some rest. She and her husband went to bed that night with heavy hearts, exhausted with worry. Sleep was impossible for Joyce, and she found herself sitting up in bed as her husband dozed fitfully. She had tossed and turned for hours, but sleep was not to come.

Suddenly she felt wide awake and alert – something was happening in that bedroom. There was a strong sensation of a presence filling the room, and there was a misty cloud forming at the foot of the bed, growing brighter by the minute. From the centre of this bright mist came a voice: 'Paul will be all right. Do not worry. Have faith.' Gradually the light and the mist cleared, and Joyce felt uplifted and supremely confident.

Shaking awake her bewildered husband, she told him excitedly that Paul was going to be fine and make a full recovery. Being a level-headed, practical man, he tried to calm Joyce, and warned her that the hospital had said no such thing, so her optimism might be totally unfounded. Joyce would not be swayed from her conviction. 'I was visited by an angel,' she told him, 'and I know for certain the message was clear, and I did not imagine or invent it. Paul will be well.'

At the hospital the following day Joyce learnt that

the doctors had reversed their decision not to treat Paul, and now wished to go ahead with chemotherapy to see if it might make a difference, although they still offered little hope. To everyone's amazement, not least the medical staff, Paul responded to treatment better than anyone's wildest dreams. All the treatment went extremely well, and his health improved in leaps and bounds. He was eventually declared clear, and came home to lead a normal life.

Today Paul is a strong young man, enjoying life to the full, and extremely grateful to the hospital staff and all who played a part in his recovery. His mother never once doubted the outcome from that special night, for she had received the message that all would be well from the highest authority of all.

Rain lashed the windows, and the damp seemed to seep under the door. Winter that year was proving to be cold and miserable for Mary. She was unwell, and getting worse by the minute. Not quite four years old, she was suffering from 'double pneumonia'. So severe did Mary's condition become that her mother was informed it was unlikely that her daughter would survive another night.

Although extremely ill and very young, Mary

nonetheless vividly recalls the events of the following night. From being weak and frail and very miserable she suddenly felt great happiness. The room was filled with the most wonderful music, unlike any she had ever heard before or since. It remains in her memory so clearly that she often finds it playing in her head.

To her delight, she then saw what she thought was a fairy in the corner of her room. She recalls a long white robe and a deep red cord around its waist. She called out to her mother to come and see, but when she arrived the figure had disappeared and nothing could be heard of the celestial music. What was clear for all to see, however, was the dramatic change in Mary's condition. Mary told her the whole story, and her mother could see how happy and excited the little girl was, and how it had brought about a miraculous change in her. For the first time in days Mary fell into a deep natural sleep, and astounded the doctor on his return with her marked improvement. He later confessed to her mother that he had held out no hope at all for her.

Mary realises how fortunate she is, and the feeling of happiness she experienced that night has for the most part remained with her. She believes that it is her mission and duty to try and spread this happiness, and has a strong sense of trying to do good and help as many people as possible. She sees this as sharing her gift from the angels, and as a way of saying thank you.

> *The angel is actually the message himself. His*
> *appearance is the message that heaven is intensely*
> *concerned with us, and that God cares for us like a*
> *father for his children.*
>
> H. C. MOOLENBURG

Artists receive inspiration from many sources. For some the countryside and nature are the primary source, whilst others need busy cities, people or even their own inner visions to help them create. Lesley feels strongly that her main source of inspiration comes from angelic sources. For many years angels have been part of her life, assisting her first of all in a quite dramatic way many years ago in Africa.

As a young woman of twenty-two she met and married a Nigerian and went to live in Nigeria, full of happiness and excitement for the future. Her family were sad and worried that she would be going to live so far away, and indeed it caused some ill feeling, to the extent that by the time she left for Africa they were not speaking to each other. Lesley then lost all contact with her family.

To Lesley's dismay, fairly quickly after her arrival her hopes for a bright future were dashed, and her dream of life in the sun turned sour. Lesley found herself feeling alienated and isolated. Her husband's job kept him travelling constantly, and she felt very vulnerable in a strange land. This isolation became acute when she found herself pregnant. When labour was due, she found herself at the hospital alone, her husband yet again far away. All this unhappiness and anxiety cannot have helped her physically, and she felt instinctively that things were going to go wrong.

Labour was indeed complicated, and at one point a drip had to be set up attached to her arm. Soon this felt extremely uncomfortable, and all signs of her condition indicated that something was seriously wrong. At this point Lesley lost consciousness, and the next thing she remembers is seeing an anxious face bending over her – the consultant obstetrician in her nightgown. Finally, with the doctor's help, Lesley gave birth to a beautiful baby girl, much to the relief of everyone.

After resting for most of the day, Lesley began to feel much better, and her baby daughter was obviously healthy and happy. She was delighted to see the doctor again, but was most surprised to hear her version of the night's events. One of a team of gynaecologists, the doctor had been working non-stop at the hospital for forty-eight hours and was completely exhausted. She went to her room, placed a 'do not disturb' notice on the door, locked it, and fell into a deep sleep.

In the early hours of the morning she felt herself being shaken awake, and heard a voice in her ear saying insistently, 'Go at once to room number 6, Mrs Ajao and her baby are dying.' She staggered to her feet grumbling, but found the door still firmly locked from the inside, and no-one in the room. Confused, she reasoned that she must have been dreaming, and went

73

back to bed gratefully sinking back beneath the sheets.

Seconds later, to her astonishment, the same thing occurred again. She was gripped even more firmly by the shoulder, shaken and urged to go to the aid of Mrs Ajao and her baby. This time she was wide awake, and to her disbelief she saw a figure in the room. It was a young woman, dressed all in white and repeating the message over and over. This time she leapt out of bed and ran down the corridor to where Lesley lay. She realised at once that a mistake had been made and the incorrect stimulant was in the liquid drip flowing into Lesley's arm. With great speed she removed the drip not a moment too soon, and Lesley and her baby were safe at last. The doctor's skill and experience then came into play, and the baby was safely delivered.

Lesley and the doctor could only agree and conclude that she had been roused by an angel that night. The doctor told her that she felt sure she and the baby had been saved for some special purpose. Lesley produces to this day the most wonderful artwork, and has had many examples throughout her life of help from a very special source. She will never forget that night however, when the doctor and her guardian angel delivered her a beautiful baby girl.

Angels have very special jobs, mainly they look after babies.

Stacey, 10

For as long as she could remember Pamela had suffered from ear, nose and throat infections. Treatment for these conditions and operations almost became a way of life. By the time she had reached the age of thirteen, the problems were very acute and it was clear that she would have to go into hospital for a long spell in an effort to clear these problems once and for all. After a stay of several weeks with Pamela's condition not improving at all, it was suggested that she should have more surgery. The problem at this point was mastoids, which were very painful.

One afternoon the nurses told Pamela that her operation would take place the following morning, but until then she had to endure the severe pain in her ears. The nurses according to their rank wore either a dark blue uniform with a starched frilly cap or a dark green one. During the day they would often receive help from nuns living at a local convent, and they of course wore mainly black.

Evening came with no respite for Pamela. The pain in her ears was so intense that she got out of bed to pace up and down in a futile attempt to take her mind off it. It grew dark, and Pamela could see the nurses in their green and navy uniforms gathered round a lamp in the little room at the end of the ward. The pain was so relentless that in desperation she threw herself to the floor and literally banged her head on it. The smell of the wood and the polish still remains when she closes her eyes and remembers that terrible night and the even worse pain. Distraught and frantic with pain she was at the end of her tether.

It was at this moment that she felt arms go around her and lift her gently from the floor. It was, she says, the strangest of sensations – not like a normal lift, but more like a floating sensation. She realised later that as a thirteen-year-old how difficult it would have been for anyone to lift her like a feather from floor level. She literally floated towards her bed and was gently placed between the sheets.

This was when she saw the figure who had come to her aid. It was dressed completely in white from head to foot. The most amazing thing, however, was that the searing pain in her ears had gone completely. Sinking into bed, Pamela fell immediately into a deep sleep. No memory of what happened next remains with Pamela, until she awoke in bed after the surgery. The operation was complete and successful. Pamela opened her eyes and asked rather hazily 'Am I still in heaven? Are you the angel?' Unamused, a rather crusty old nurse answered a sharp 'No indeed' to both questions and added, 'Go back to sleep girl.'

Over the years Pamela has deliberated the events of that night and reasons that a single nurse would definitely have not been able to lift her in one movement from the floor, so effortlessly. There was not a single member of staff who wore white, all the uniforms being very dark in colour. Who was the mysterious figure in white? Why did the awful pain disappear in an instant? She has come to her own conclusions, but one thing is certain: if ever a child needed help from the angels, Pamela did that night.

Amy's mother exclaimed with frustration, 'It could only happen to us!' Every time they went on holiday, some accident or illness seemed to befall them. This year Amy was the victim. She had been playing cricket on the beach all morning with her parents and two brothers, and worked up a hearty appetite. A picnic lunch had been arranged by their mother, and they sat down to enjoy it. To everyone's surprise, Amy declined any food saying she felt a little sickly and had tummy ache. It was unlike Amy to refuse food, and it was at this point that her mother uttered those words of doom. Seeking directions to the local hospital, they swiftly got Amy to the casualty department. The diagnosis took no time at all; it was very clearly appendicitis, and Amy was admitted. The useless appendage would have to be removed at once.

There was poor Amy not halfway through her holiday, sitting in a hospital ward in a strange town. Gradually she started to feel better but decidedly fed up, since the weather was now improving. At one point, alone in her room, she felt so sad that she started to cry.

At that moment a movement above the door lintel made her glance upwards, lifting her head. There above the lintel were two tiny cherubs, each surrounded by an intense white light. Amy stared captivated, and felt a strong glow of love surround her. They were so beautiful that she was sad when only seconds later they were gone, leaving the little room to its mellow light once more. Amy did not know what to think, but she did know she now felt very happy indeed, and all her misery had completely vanished.

Her family arrived full of chatter and news, but Amy could not bring herself to tell them what had happened to her. It felt very special and private, and she was sure her brothers would simply laugh at her. It was some considerable time later when she and her mother were alone that she plucked up the courage to tell her the story. Her mother smiled and said 'Well, you were very poorly for a while, dear.' Amy felt that her mother believed her to have imagined the whole thing, but she knows deep down that this was not so. It is only now, ten years later, that she feels she can tell her story.

In the last chapter, we discussed the link between yellow roses and St Theresa. The following story contains elements of this association in a rather dramatic way.

Holly lay in bed, her face burning, and shivering at the same time. Her throat hurt, and she had not a grain of energy. Jane had never seen her little girl so poorly, and the doctor had to call on a house visit. He was kind and reassuring, and gave Holly something to help reduce her high temperature. It was the early hours of the morning before Holly finally fell asleep, and by that time Jane was exhausted. She could not help but worry despite the doctor's comforting words. She mopped her daughter's brow, for she was still very hot indeed, but at least she was getting some sleep, Jane thought.

Realising that she had not eaten all day Jane went down to the kitchen to prepare a snack and make a cup of tea. Climbing the stairs to check on Holly, and taking her drink with her, she was startled by Holly's voice shouting, 'Mummy!' Dashing to Holly's room, Jane was astonished to see her daughter sitting up in bed smiling. Most amazing of all, Holly pointed to the bedside table. 'Look what the lovely lady gave me,' she said, and there was a single yellow rose!

There seemed to be no logical explanation as to how it got there. The only surety was that Holly was definitely better, and she feels the woman in the long white dress who gave her such a beautiful present must have had something to do with it.

Martin was a happy baby, who filled the house with giggles. Soon it would be his first birthday, an occasion they all looked forward to. Just before his birthday Martin came down with a heavy cold, and Patricia had never seen him look so miserable. He did not improve, and a couple of days later, after trying all the usual child medications, they called the doctor.

The doctor advised a hospital admission, and on arrival a diagnosis of chest infection was announced. Patricia was frightened; her much loved son looked very poorly and seemed to be getting worse. His breathing was laboured, and he could scarcely open his eyes. He was in good hands, however, and was receiving the best treatment available.

Making her way down the hospital corridor to the coffee machine, Patricia felt as if this was all unreal, some bad dream from which she would wake any minute. Her husband had gone home for a few hours' rest and would be back shortly. Walking wearily back to Martin's room, she opened door and was gripped with fear. Standing over the cot was a figure, surrounded by a mist. She could not move, but gradually her fear subsided as the light around the figure increased and she felt a strong feeling of love fill the tiny room.

The figure slowly melted away. Her little boy was still safe and sleeping peacefully. What could it all mean? Martin recovered slowly and steadily, and was eventually allowed home. Patricia told her husband what she had seen, but he dismissed the story, saying Patricia had been overwrought. She will not accept this, however, and says she is certain of what she saw and feels convinced that it was an angel of healing.

Angels fly down from the sky to take care of you when you are poorly.
SAMANTHA, 5

5

Comfort and Reassurance

hildren need all the hugs they can get. A hug is
comforting and reassuring, a certain signal that
they are loved, often when words are difficult.
For adults a hug conjures up times in infancy when one
was wrapped in a blanket, had a knee scrape attended
to, or was tucked up in bed on a cold winter night. At
least as adults we are certain most of the time about the
source of our anxieties. This is not always the case for
children, who pick up adults' anxieties without any
understanding or ability to analyse what is happening.

Laura found herself in this situation one evening.
Whilst most adults dread the sound of an ambulance or
fire engine, most children find the loud noise and flash-
ing light decidedly exciting. Laura and her brother had
always thought so until the night an ambulance was
called to their home – and it was no fun at all.

The evening meal was over, and the children were
getting ready for bed. Laura's father, who would normally have read a story to the children at this point,

declined saying he was not feeling very well. He announced that he would go to bed shortly and have an early night, certain that it would solve his problem and that he would feel right as rain by morning. Laura's mother supervised the bedtime routine, and was about to give the children a drink when her husband complained of feeling much worse. At this point he had developed chest pains and looked very white. Laura's mother acted fast and called for an ambulance. She then called for their grandmother to hold the fort whilst she accompanied her husband to hospital. Laura was picking up her mother's fear, and started to tremble as her grandmother arrived.

Next morning Laura was surprised to see a pale-faced mother making breakfast. 'I have to go back to the hospital soon,' she told them, 'but first I wanted to talk to you and explain what happened.' She told them as simply as possible that their father had suffered a heart attack, he was being looked after by some very special people, and they were not to worry because she felt sure he would be well again soon. Their grandmother had said she would stay as long as she was needed and they were not to worry.

At this point Laura said with a slight tone of exasperation, 'I know Daddy will be well, and I am not worrying because the lady told me not to.' 'Which lady?' her mother asked, confused. 'The lady who kissed me goodnight,' Laura replied. 'Do you mean Grandma?' her mother asked, still deeply puzzled.

'No,' Laura emphasised, 'the pretty lady in the long white dress and a bright light, she told me Daddy would be well.'

Silence fell on the little kitchen. Laura's mother and grandmother exchanged glances, and then her mother came over to Laura and gave her a hug. Her eyes were full of tears, and in truth she did not know what to think. The fact remains, however, that Laura's father did indeed make a full recovery. Now, some fifteen years later, Laura believes she was reassured by her guardian angel.

Carrying a secret and being unable to share it with anyone is a source of anxiety and depression, and for Molly this had been particularly acute.

Lying in bed she heard the car sweep up the gravel drive, its wheels crunching to a halt. The doorbell was pressed with some urgency and irritation. It was to no avail, Molly felt pinned to the bed and no amount of ringing on the doorbell would rouse her. She could almost feel the irritation seeping under the door and picture the cross face. The car sped away, and all was silent again. A huge sigh escaped from deep within Molly, depression hung over her like a fog, and her grief was virtually palpable. The afternoon wore on and still she lay on the bed, motionless and unable to move.

She remembered the time when she was a lively girl of fifteen, living in a tiny village in rural Ireland. The most excitement she had ever known was the day the fair and showband arrived. The fair people were the most glamorous and sparkling individuals she had ever met, and she was captivated by the whole scene. In particular, she was captivated by a bright-eyed youth for the duration of the visit. Soon it was time for the fair to leave, and Molly was felt devastated. Eventually, to her dismay, she discovered she was also pregnant. In rural Ireland all those years ago it was indeed catastrophic, and she felt she could tell no-one. Her parents would have been dismayed and furious, dreading the scandal in the village.

Eventually she plucked up the courage to tell the village priest, the only option, she felt, open to her. He was kind and sympathetic, but urged her to tell no-one until he had time to make arrangements. It was decided that she would go to be cared for by a group of nuns in a convent as far away as possible from her home. When the baby had been delivered, they would try and find her employment. Arrangements were duly made, and Molly left the village for the convent. Family and friends were told that a place had been secured for her in service with a large wealthy family in Dublin. When the baby was born, the nuns did find

Molly a job in service with a family in Dublin who were prepared to take the baby as well.

Time passed, and Molly was settling into her new life well. Life was determined to stretch Molly to the extremes, however. One day when the baby was only just over three months old, Molly went to her cot one morning to find her still and lifeless – the child had died during the night. Molly was distraught and inconsolable, firmly believing that this was punishment for her sin.

She remained in service for many years before she finally returned to her home village, the secret still firmly locked inside her. Eventually she married a farmer, and in time had two more children who grew fit and healthy. They were of course a source of great pleasure, but the guilt and the depression surrounding the events of her dead baby's short life would not go away. The bouts of depression became more frequent and of longer duration, until here she was lying on her bed some thirty years later, still suffering. The room grew dark, and still Molly lay pinned on her bed. This, she thought, is what people mean when they talk about the depth of despair.

From deep within her, and with such a force it frightened her, she yelled at the top of her voice, 'How long, dear God?' In an instant, the room filled with a bright intense light. Molly sat bolt upright in bed. The light filled the whole room by now, and the feeling of love was overpowering. From the centre of this light emerged a large and very beautiful angel. Most amazing of all for Molly was that the angel held a baby in her arms. Both faces radiated a smile towards Molly, sending love and forgiveness. Molly felt the burden of those thirty years lift from her shoulders. She knew she was forgiven and freed from guilt. That day she had peeped into Paradise.

You might think that someone who had experienced angel visitations on a regular basis would have little trouble describing these events to others. Not so for Caroline – her most difficult problem was in fact how to tell her nearest and dearest. From early childhood Caroline knew she possessed psychic gifts. Certain events, mundane or dramatic, would be known to her before they had happened. She would have strong premonitions, and as she grew older they seemed to become more frequent. Many moments in her life have been what one could term angel encounters. These would range from a warm glow to tingling sensations, bright lights, and actual meetings with angels.

Not wishing to frighten her children, Caroline had given them broad hints without going into detail, always giving them the idea that they did indeed have a guardian angel whom they could contact if they should ever feel alone. One day whilst casually chatting, Caroline was delighted when they started to ask specific questions about spiritual matters and angels in particular. She answered as informatively as she knew how, and was pleased by the timing, because she was aware that a well loved aunt was terminally ill. The children would be most distressed when they eventually discovered this, and perhaps this conversation might make things easier.

The aunt died not long after, and Caroline comforted the children by explaining that she felt with certainty that she was happy and in heaven. As she spoke to the children, a tingling sensation filled her entire body and she felt instinctively that this was the aunt communicating and confirming what she had told them.

During the next few months when Caroline thought about her aunt or missed her especially, the warm tingling would often occur. She decided the time was right to tell the girls, and sitting them down one day she explained that she felt certain the aunt was communicating through this tingling sensation. Far from being frightened, the girls were fascinated. One daughter asked her mother if on the next occasion their aunt communicated with her and they were there, would she tell them. 'Certainly,' said Caroline, pleased with their reaction.

Both sisters had their birthday in the same month,

and usually a family outing or special treat would be organised. This year a trip to a musical was arranged. Driving to the theatre the children were very excited but one of them pointed out that normally their aunt would have been with them. As they found their seats she remarked, 'I do wish auntie was here for our birthday treats.' 'I am sure she knows you miss her and are thinking of her today,' Caroline replied. Sitting in their seats they all felt happy anticipation as the orchestra began to play.

At this moment, Caroline felt the familiar tingle spread through her hands, and thought how wonderful that even here in the theatre her aunt was communicating. Remembering her promise to the girls, she suddenly had an idea. Reaching out in the darkness she took a hand of each of her daughters into hers. Their faces lit up, and with eyes like saucers they said they could both feel the tingling. It had been transferred to them. One of the girls whispered to her mother, 'Isn't it wonderful that auntie is here after all!'

The Baker family were going abroad for the first time to stay in a rented French farmhouse. At the end of the first day, their daughter Charlotte said goodnight to her mother and went to bed. Janet and her husband discovered how to open the patio doors, and took their drinks into the garden to enjoy the fresh country air. Turning to her husband, Janet said, 'This is going to be a wonderful holiday.' At this point a wail reached them from upstairs. 'You spoke too soon,' said her husband, and Janet nodded, getting up to go and see what the matter was.

Charlotte was sitting up in bed sobbing. Janet was confused. 'What's the problem?' she asked. 'Where is my lady?' Charlotte said. 'Does she know we're in France?' Her mother had no idea what she was talking about, so she sat down patiently and asked Charlotte to explain. Gradually the story began to unfold, while Janet could only listen wide-eyed. It emerged that some time ago, when Charlotte was back home in England, she had been afraid of the dark. Janet recalls the period and how they had to coax her to bed on several occasions, but also how it had seemed she lost the fear as quickly as it had come.

Charlotte told Janet that one night a lovely lady in a long white dress had stood in the corner of her room and told Charlotte not to be afraid. Every night since, the lady had appeared briefly, and Charlotte would fall asleep at once knowing she would watch over her. Her distress was because now they were in France, she was unsure how her lady would know where she was.

Janet could scarcely believe what she was hearing, but Charlotte's distress was real enough. She held her daughter's hand, and said she was sure that the angel lady (for it seemed to her that was what she was) would certainly know where they were, and watch over her even if she could not be seen. Content with this explanation, the little girl went to sleep. She was never frightened of the dark again, but she also says that she never saw her 'lady' again either.

For every soul there is a guardian watching it.
THE QUR'AN

It had been a long day for Julia. Her feet ached, and she could feel the beginnings of a migraine. Longing to be home, she locked the door of her florist shop, and jumped into her car. She still had to collect her daughter from a friend's house before she could go home and start the evening meal. She found Alice waiting for her, full of the day's news.

Home at last, Julia parked the car in the drive and opened the front door, wearily switching on the light. Gasping in disbelief, she looked around at the mess which greeted her. Someone had broken in and completely ransacked the tiny flat. Not a great deal had been taken, but the mess was awful – drawers and cupboards emptied all over the floor and lots of broken glass from the window where entry had been gained. Julia tried hard to control her mounting panic for Alice's sake, but it was not easy.

Months passed and although they were more or less back to normal, Julia was still full of fear every time she put her key in the lock. One evening she found the problem quite overwhelming, and sitting at the kitchen table she began to cry. Her daughter was in the lounge watching television, and to Julia's relief had shown no sign of fear herself.

Alice came in and saw her mother crying, and said in a very earnest voice, 'Mummy, you mustn't worry, we shall never have burglars again.' Smiling through her tears, Julia decided to humour her daughter. 'Of course not,' she said, 'I am being silly. The policeman will keep an eye on our flat now.' 'No,' said Alice. 'It's not the policeman that is watching over us, it's the angel.' Julia stared at her daughter. 'What do you mean?' she asked. Alice told her in a very matter-of-fact voice that several weeks ago, not long after the break-in, she had woken up and gone into the kitchen for a drink. Standing in the tiny hallway was an angel, filling the whole area with light. Slowly the angel faded, and Alice knew she had come to watch over them and protect them. No-one would ever break into their home again.

Julia was speechless. Alice had not even mentioned this to her, but had shown no sign of fear at this apparition, only confident acceptance. Puzzled, and yet never doubting her daughter's word, she gave her a big kiss. It is worth noting that five years on they are still safe and secure in their flat.

Protection of the vulnerable is common in angel encounters. There are similarities between the last story and that of Stella, another young mother who feels especially helped.

It had all started so well Stella thought. She and Simon seemed so happy and well-suited that life was very pleasant indeed. Simon worked mainly from home, and one day asked if Stella thought it was a good idea to move out of the city to the country, where life would be more peaceful and less expensive. Stella agreed, and any reservations she might have had melted after the move, as spring turned into a hot summer.

Autumn arrived and with it came the birth of Daniel. Life was smooth and Stella content, believing herself to be a very fortunate woman indeed. Life progressed quickly even at the slower rural pace, and soon it was Daniel's fifth birthday.

Only weeks after Daniel's birthday, Stella's life fell apart. Simon told her he would be leaving permanently. He had formed a relationship with someone else on his increasingly frequent trips to London, and would be moving back to the city. The nagging doubts she had tried to block from her mind were confirmed, but she was still shocked by Simon's announcement.

Leafy quiet lanes turned into sinister walkways as the days grew shorter, winter approached and Stella's perspective on her once idyllic home changed dramatically. Loneliness and fear became part of her everyday life, as well as a feeling of sheer helplessness in the isolated cottage. Trying to be cheerful for Daniel's sake was a great strain, but she told herself that she must hide her anxiety from him. Children, of course, are not so easily hoodwinked, and Daniel was only too aware of his mother's fears.

One very dark winter evening Stella and Daniel walked home down the dark lane. It was very frosty, and the dead leaves crunched underfoot. The sound echoed slightly, and Stella became convinced that they were being followed. By the time they reached the house she was shaking, and struggled to get the key in the lock. Switching on all the lights in the house she went into the kitchen to busy herself with the evening meal, trying to control her nerves and appear casual in front of Daniel.

The little boy eyed her intently. 'You mustn't worry, Mummy,' he said. Stella handed him a mug of hot chocolate, astonished to see such a kind, caring expression on the little boy's face. 'I will try not to be so silly,' she said. 'Good,' Daniel replied, 'because you must have seen our angel.' Stella's jaw dropped open. 'Angel?' she repeated. Taking Stella's hand, he dragged her outside. 'Look, there on the roof,' he said, pointing up. 'She is looking after us.'

Stella could see nothing, only the dark roof. 'Are you all right now, Mummy?' Daniel asked in a very grown-up manner. 'Yes, of course I am,' she replied. 'And we will of course be fine.' After all, she thought, if Daniel could see a guardian angel, who was she to disagree.

Angels appear in all sorts of places when one would least expect them, often disguised as normal people in modern-day dress. This is perhaps to ensure that they do not startle the person involved, particularly a child. Our next story is most unusual, and involves an angel obviously concerned with a child's acceptance of the supernatural.

Do sunshine, white sand, palm trees and blue skies make you think of angels? I think not, even though I am sure angels are found all over the world. We are so conditioned to think of angels revealing themselves at night in conjunction with starry skies, that to see one on a hot day in an exotic location seems incongruous.

Melody and her mother were enjoying a much awaited holiday in Australia, and hoped to travel a little further afield whilst on holiday for six weeks. Their story begins in Perth, Western Australia. After some time in this beautiful city they were wondering where to go from there, and several people had suggested Bali. Although Melody's mother was a little nervous at the prospect, she decided to take the plunge. Having booked the flight, she was disconcerted to find that accommodation would be a problem.

They found their way to a local travel agent, but there was nothing he could do. It was the height of the tourist season, and every reasonably priced hotel was full. Melody's mother was at a loss as to what to do next. They had the flights arranged and little idea as to an alternative, even unsure as to their position if they should cancel the proposed trip. This was not a life-threatening situation, but for a mother and her eleven-year-old daughter travelling alone, it was stressful.

However, Melody said to her mother perfectly calmly that she could see a man sitting on the sofa in their apartment. Where he had come from she had no idea, but her mother could see nobody. Her daughter said the man had told her that he had come to help, and they were not to worry. He was dressed in normal, modern-day clothing, and had a calm, reassuring air about him. He told Melody to have faith in him, that all would be well, and that they should not try and cancel their flights. Melody said thank you, and with that he disappeared.

Melody's mother was confused, but found herself also saying thank you, even though she could see nobody. An atmosphere of calm settled in the apartment, and both mother and daughter felt peaceful. What the solution might be, however, was not yet apparent. A little while later, the phone rang, and it was the travel agent. He sounded as surprised as Melody's mother when he told them that a vacancy had arisen, in a lovely, well-positioned hotel, ideal for their needs. It was a most unusual occurrence at that time of the year, he said, but it would be perfect.

A very happy girl and her mother set off for the airport, full of confidence that they had a very special agent of their very own.

*Angels don't have legs, they don't need them with such
big wings. They fly everywhere around the world
helping people.*

SAM, 5

Jenny was a dancer of considerable talent, and ballet held a particular fascination for her. At the age of ten she lived to dance, and was determined that this would be her chosen life. She worked hard, and had earned a place in a reputable if small ballet company. Jenny's parents were very supportive, committing themselves financially and time-wise to her interests.

One Christmas the main theatre in Jenny's home town planned to produce a lavish pantomime. Leading parts would be played by well-known TV celebrities, mainly from children's television, and the casting director approached the ballet school to offer roles to their pupils. The entire school was in a state of high excitement, not least Jenny, who fervently hoped to have a substantial part. Rehearsals started, and Jenny found to her delight that she was dancing in a small section with just two other girls, where their talents were sure to be noticed.

Days before the opening night, Jenny's excitement was nearing fever pitch, and she was having to be pushed hard to go to bed and get some sleep. Singing louder than ever one night as she took her bath, she leaped out of the bath, wrapped her towel around her, and pirouetted towards the door. Exactly how it happened she never did come to terms with, but she slipped and fell awkwardly, yelling with pain as she hit the bathroom floor.

Her mother could only weep in sympathy as her father drove them to casualty. Casualty staff, however, told them it was not really as bad as they had feared. Jenny had suffered a bad sprain, but nothing had been broken. Nevertheless, it was the end of her pantomime involvement, and Jenny was near to despair. Back home there was only rest. Her ankle was throbbing and Jenny knew there would be little chance of sleep that night.

After a long time lying down thinking about the events of the evening and trying to cope with the discomfort, Jenny sat up in bed and switched on the bedside lamp. It was a little cold in the bedroom, and that along with the depressing thought of all she would be missing made her shiver. With a start, she realised that she was not alone in the room. At the foot of her bed was the figure of a young girl, much the same age as herself, but surrounded by a bright glow. Her dress appeared to shimmer and was pale blue in colour. A feeling of love and warmth flowed from this figure, and Jenny felt no fear, only elation.

Gradually the figure faded, and Jenny found herself in a state of contentment and very sleepy. Sliding down between the sheets, she slipped into a much needed deep sleep. The next morning her mother came into her room with a drink, and expressed surprise that she had managed to sleep so well. To the surprise of Jenny and her parents, the throbbing pain in her ankle had gone and the swelling was greatly reduced. Over breakfast Jenny told the story of the visit she had had the previous night. It was greeted as these stories so often are with the answer: 'Just a dream; you were overwrought.' Jenny insisted that she had not even been to sleep at that point but had been sitting up in bed with the light on. Her parents did not know how to react and decided to keep their counsel.

Recovery was astonishingly swift, and although Jenny missed the opening night, she was well enough after a check-up at the hospital to join the cast for the rest of the pantomime run. It was some fifteen years ago that this happened, and today Jenny is a successful dancer. She says the memory of that night has never diminished in its clarity, and she feels sure the healing process was speeded by the angel's visit. Since that time a feeling of protection has remained with her and a certain sense of 'what will be, will be.'

Children and Angels

*Angels have special round things on their heads. They
use them to make you better.*

LAURA, 5

If a list were compiled of the things children are most
afraid of, the dark would definitely be near the top.
Through the ages children have demanded light at
night to help allay their fears.

Jean and her sister slept together in a huge brass
bed. Both sisters were afraid of the dark, and they were
allowed a candle placed in a saucer of water on the bedside table. Unfortunately this only made things much
worse, because flickering shadows cast on the walls
scared them even more.

At about the age of seven, Jean was a bright, sensi-
ble child. She and her sister attended Sunday school
regularly, and paid attention to all they were told. They
decided that when they felt afraid of the dark, they
would sing one of the lovely hymns they had learnt at
Sunday school. Jean suggested they sing:

> *Lord keep me safe this night*
> *Secure from all my fears*
> *May angels guard me while I sleep*
> *Till morning light appears*

Each night they sang this verse and felt considerably
calmer, and then they would go to sleep.

One night after singing this hymn, Jean felt a sudden

compulsion to turn her head and look behind her. On the brass rail behind them were the shadows of two angels. They were clearly two young girls, one with long wavy hair, the other with slightly shorter hair. Jean points out here that she and her sister had very short, bobbed hair, so they were obviously not their own shadows. The silhouettes had large wings, spreading wide in a protective gesture.

Jean experienced a sensation of great happiness and security spreading through her. Giving her little sister a shake, she exclaimed 'They have come!' Neither sister showed any surprise, for as Jean said, 'We had asked for angels to guard us, and angels we got!' Knowing finally that there was nothing to fear and feeling perfectly safe, they fell into peaceful sleep.

In telling of their experience, the usual standard reply greeted them: 'Just a dream, dear.' Jean puts forward the following arguments. Firstly she says the angels appeared as shadows to prevent them being afraid, since shadows would be easier to cope with than a full-blown angel. Secondly, the candle was well to the right-hand side of the bed and would not have cast shadows behind their heads. Thirdly, the silhouettes were solid and unwavering, not flickering like other shadows cast by the candle. Had it been a dream, is it likely that both sisters would have had identical ones?

The story has an interesting twist. Many years later Jean became a grandmother, and frequently took photographs of her grandchildren. One night her two granddaughters were ready for bed, and Jean took a photograph. They wore white nightdresses and had long hair, one very long and wavy, the other slightly shorter. When the photograph was developed Jean was struck by the amazing similarity between her own 'angels' in the photograph and the angels who visited the sisters so long ago.

We have all seen on our TV screens and in our newspapers the faces of frightened children who live in a war zone. No matter how distressed we may be by those images, we cannot possibly understand exactly what it must be like for them. There are many people in Britain today, however, who clearly recall being a child in the Second World War and some of the resulting fear. James remembers the period very well indeed. As a twelve-year-old he had a full grasp of the situation. As a London firefighter, James's father was in a highly dangerous position, and his occupation frequently led him into hair-raising situations. There was little time to consider one's personal safety during the Blitz, and a swift reaction was essential.

One night during the early days of the Blitz James and his mother went to stay with a friend. They reasoned that there might be safety in numbers, or at least comfort and company. Trying to sleep in a new bed and a strange house was not easy, and fear was very strong at that moment. It was then that James became aware of what he describes as a presence, which made him sit up sharply in bed. He was wide awake and conscious that the bedroom door was open, and he had a full view of the hall outside, which was bathed in a glowing light. James stared, trying to take in the scene. In the centre of this light he saw a beautiful young woman. Above her head was a luminous halo of light, and in one hand she held what James describes as a beacon. It was the most wonderful sight and lasted some five seconds before dissolving along with the glow, until gradually the hall was dark again.

Mulling over these events for some considerable time afterwards, James tried to collect his thoughts. His fear and anxiety had vanished, and he felt only calmness and peace. He eventually drifted off to sleep feeling extremely happy.

The following day James related the whole encounter to his mother who did not (unusually) tell him it was just a dream. She listened very carefully and then said she would visit the local spiritualists' meeting to see if anyone could give her an explanation. The people at the meeting all agreed that James had been a witness to something very wonderful, and felt sure this was a message of great significance – possibly that they would all be perfectly safe for the duration of the war.

Despite the years of danger that followed and the many frightening events they were subjected to, they did indeed all come through completely unscathed. James is convinced that what he saw that night was a guardian angel. He will never forget how reassuring she was, how comforting and how lovely.

We all need to feel valued, appreciated and loved. If these needs are not met, life is cold and extremely difficult, especially for a child. Karen had felt unloved and isolated as a young girl. She now realises the symptoms provoked by this state were those of depression. She felt totally engulfed by unhappiness, based even at that tender age in the knowledge that she was unloved.

At the age of five Karen needed to visit the dentist. A general anaesthetic was administered, and due to complications she came close to losing her life. However, during this crisis she had the most extraordinary experience.

She recalls with great clarity seeing many angels and communicating with them, and being told that at this point she had a choice to make. Staying with the angels was one option, and since she was surrounded by glowing light radiating pure love (a feeling she had never known), the temptation to say yes instantly was great. The second option was of course to go back to her own life on earth, but this time with the knowledge that there was something else, and that she was loved.

She returned still glowing and convinced that this glow of love would stay with her. Growing older of course meant that external influences became greater, and inevitably the glow diminished until she found the old feelings of depression and anxiety returning. Studying for her exams became difficult, since she felt confused as to which direction she should take and haunted again by feelings of being unloved. For some time she had tried meditation to calm herself and from time to time this proved to be a great help. One day when study was proving to be almost impossible, Karen decided to meditate for a while in order to calm her mind.

Almost at once she was flooded and surrounded with the same intense light she had experienced all those years ago. The warmth and love emanating from that light was, she says, almost beyond description. It was as if the emptiness inside her had been filled to the brim with love. Astonishingly, at the same time she had an overwhelming sense of knowledge. All her strivings for direction and self-awareness were banished, and she knew with clarity which direction she must take.

As the light faded, Karen sat evaluating her life until the answer came to her loud and clear. She had to cease her introspection and look outside herself. She must love others in order to be loved. Giving out love would result in receiving love – a weighty lesson for a fifteen-year-old. Her chosen path was to be nursing. Meditation continues to help Karen, now a happy and contented nurse. Creative writing has also become a vital part of her life. Most importantly, she feels enrichment and fulfilment, and her inner angel shines for all to see.

> *It can in no sense be said that heaven is outside anyone. It is within.*
> EMANUEL SWEDENBORG

There are books published of people's last words. Some of these are funny, some full of courage and wisdom, but none I believe can surpass the words of my own father. Holding his hand during what were to be his final minutes of consciousness, I was overcome with the awful prospect of losing him. He said I must always remember that the only way one could be separated from a loved one was if you ceased to love them. As long as love was constant, so was the connection. Those words steered me through the grief and have helped others too. They came to me again vividly as I heard Suzanne's story.

As children Suzanne and Mark were inseparable friends. When Mark started school, Suzanne missed him terribly, but a year later she joined him at the local junior school and settled in happily knowing he was there. She was therefore shattered to learn when she was seven years old that Mark would be leaving the area, since his father had been given a promotion that entailed a move to another part of the country. Worse was to come. Shortly after the move, Mark was involved in a road accident on his bicycle and was killed.

Years passed, and inevitably the tragedy faded, but from time to time Suzanne found herself thinking of Mark. She became convinced that on occasions, for a split second, she saw his image out of the corner of her eye, but dismissed it as imagination. Deciding her career would be in teaching, she gained a place at teacher training college, made good friends and had a busy social life.

One day some friends persuaded her to attend a festival of Mind, Body and Spirit. On impulse she sat down before a clairvoyant and listened, fascinated, to her words, as she spoke of many things which would make an impact in the following years. Eventually the woman told her that she had a guardian angel, and asked if she was aware of this. Suzanne looked confused. 'Your angel takes the form of a young boy,' she said. 'He is very close, and I'm getting a picture of him in my mind.' Suzanne could scarcely believe her ears as the description fitted Mark's appearance exactly. 'How wonderful,' she thought. 'We are not separated after all.'

Today women have more choices than ever before, and sometimes this leads to confusion. Career women face a dilemma when motherhood enters the frame. Sally faced this dilemma when at the age of thirty-five and in an important and rewarding job, she and her husband decided that it was now time to have children if they were ever going to. She finally decided that she would take a long break and then return to her career. All went smoothly at first, and they were thrilled to be the parents of a healthy baby boy, but nothing had prepared Sally for the routine and problems of motherhood.

One day was particularly fraught, as the baby cried almost incessantly from early morning until evening. Sally was beside herself. Her husband could not be reached as he was driving home and would not arrive until the early hours. Panic set in. Was the baby seriously ill, or was he simply uncomfortable? Should she ring a doctor? Should she disturb a friend?

Rushing into the kitchen quite at a loss, she poured herself a strong cup of coffee and found herself praying: 'Please God, what should I do? Help me!' In virtually an instant the baby ceased crying. Sally was stunned. Putting her coffee down, she ran to the nursery. There she stopped in her tracks, for the most

108

fantastic sight met her gaze. Beside the little cot stood a huge angel. The light emanating from this figure lit the whole room. It shimmered and appeared almost translucent in appearance.

How long she stood there, trying to take this sight in, she could not guess, but it could only have been minutes at the longest, though it felt like a lifetime. She was so elated and full of awe that she would remember it to her dying day. The angel slowly faded away. Sally was filled with a sense of comfort, knowing she was never alone and most definitely loved. What about the baby whilst all this was taking place? Well, he fell into a deep sleep, of course.

An angel appearance would not be suitable for children of a timid disposition. Andrea was timid, and at times painfully shy, which could be a real problem. It was only with her immediate family that she felt completely relaxed. There were moments when her mother would lose patience with her and came close to exasperation, although she was only too aware that the child had little control over her problem.

The day Mrs Porter moved into the house next door was to be a life-changing day for Andrea. Mrs Porter was not just a very kind elderly lady but a former teacher of children with special needs, and as such possessed an infinite amount of insight and patience. Before long Andrea found she could chat away to her new friend and was completely at ease.

In time Andrea was allowed to call her friend 'Auntie Beatie'. She learnt that Mr Porter had died and that the little house Auntie Beatie had come to live in was to help her make a fresh start after her retirement. Aunt Beatie had never been a mother herself but adored children, particularly Andrea. The years brought all sorts of problems for Andrea, not least homework, and once again Aunt Beatie was a godsend. How everyone had coped without her was a mystery.

It was a dreadful day when Andrea's mother discovered that their friend and neighbour was seriously ill, suffering from malignant and inoperable cancer. Nothing it seemed could be done, save for making her comfortable in the form of care and pain relief. The inevitable eventually happened, and Aunt Beatie died. They all missed her, especially Andrea who felt at this time that most of her self-confidence came directly from Aunt Beatie's support and advice. What she would do from here on without her mentor Andrea had no idea.

That autumn the first day of the new term in a new school arrived. It was not too bad a day all in all, but Andrea was dismayed to find even on the first evening that she would have to get down to homework. Sitting at the desk in her room she felt a gloom descend – it all felt so overpowering. Seriously doubting her ability to cope, she felt tears start to sting her eyes. Virtually at the same instant, she felt the sensation of a hand on her shoulder gently pressing and reassuring. Twisting around in her chair, she fully expected to see her mother standing behind her, having walked in without her knowledge. The door was firmly shut, and save for herself the room completely empty.

There was of course only one possible explanation, she thought – Aunt Beatie is watching over me still. Andrea felt elated and the confidence rushed back into her. I can cope, she thought, and what's more I will. Whether or not the hand on her shoulder was her old friend in the form of an angel, she would never know – but always believed this to be true.

Our last story of reassurance comes from another little girl but one far from shy. Anna was perky, chatty and full of beans, as her mother would tell her. She was adored by her parents and her big brother who was ten years her elder. Often her brother Steven would take her to the park or on shopping trips, during which he would always buy some little treat or other for her.

It was with a wail of grief therefore that Anna greeted the news that Steven was going away. They had an uncle and aunt living in Canada, who had invited Steven to go and stay should he wish to. It would fit into Steven's plans perfectly, since he had always planned to take a year's break between school and university, and if he could find a job he would then have a little financial security. The whole family apart from Anna thought it a wonderful opportunity. Waving goodbye at the airport was quite traumatic for the seven-year-old, since a year sounded like a lifetime to her.

In time postcards arrived, and Anna loved them. Receiving mail was a novelty and a great source of excitement. It certainly helped ease the pain that Steven was so far away. The year rolled on, and soon Steven had been in Canada for eight months. Anna's mother told her it would not be too long before he would be home again.

Lying in bed, Anna looked at all the postcards on her bedroom bulletin board and thought how wonderful they were. Maybe one day I shall go to Canada too, she mused. Gradually she drifted off to sleep, thoughts of adventure and travel filling her head. What made her suddenly wake she had no idea, but wake she did and with great suddenness. At first she wondered where she was, because her bedroom was full of light. She recalls that this was the brightest light she had ever seen and yet quite gentle and comforting to watch.

This light filled the room for several minutes before fading and leaving Anna in darkness once more. Puzzled and confused she went into her parents' bedroom and waking them told them what had happened. Her father was a little grumpy, and pointed out that it was two o'clock in the morning. Anna's mother gently led her back to bed and told her not to worry and go back to sleep.

The following day they received a phone call from the aunt in Canada, saying that they were not to worry but Steven had been involved in a road accident. He had been travelling in a car with some friends, and they had been hit head on by a speeding stolen car. He was in hospital, but his injuries were not life-threatening though they would require a longish spell in the orthopaedic ward.

At the end of this long reassuring conversation, Anna's mother asked when exactly the crash had taken place. The aunt worked out the time difference and answered, 'It would have been about two o'clock in the morning in Britain.' Putting down the receiver, Anna's mother told them what the aunt had said. All three looked at each other for a moment, and then Anna said, 'That explains the light, doesn't it? The angels were telling me Steven would be all right.' Her parents could only nod in agreement.

6

Messages from Beyond the Grave

We have many accounts of angels rescuing children from danger and appearing when they are dangerously ill. Unfortunately, not all children survive serious illness and many families have to face the trauma of losing a child. One of the most distressing aspects of a child dying is that the parents can no longer picture where they are. They will be told time and again that the child has gone to a better place, or more specifically that they are now in heaven. What a blessing it would be if all grieving parents had assurance that this was really the case.

Looking back in history, it is interesting to note that art began to depict cherubs in increasing numbers around the time of the Black Death. There would have been few households at that time that had not lost at least one child to the disease. What a comfort it must have been then to see these cherub paintings and sculptures enabling the parents to imagine their child was now an angel. Similarly in Victorian times when chest ailments and enteritis caused the death of many children, we see depictions of angels everywhere, especially as marble statues in graveyards.

The very words 'children' and 'heaven' in one sentence provoke an emotional reaction. Emanuel Swedenborg teaches that all children go to heaven and in their state of innocence become angels there. He communicated for a period of twenty-five years with angelic sources, and wrote all he was told for others to read. I have received letters and newspaper reports from various parts of the globe stating that children immediately prior to death have discussed heaven, and claimed that they have seen angels.

A family in the USA lost a four-year-old girl to degenerative heart disease. Her mother states that the child would frequently talk about heaven, telling them about visions she had had illustrating the afterlife. How or why, her mother asks, would a little girl make up such stories? Each grieving parent must wish that their child could communicate and tell them they were happy. It may sound like an impossible dream, but this is exactly what happened to the family grieving for their son Michael.

Judy and her family were devastated by the death of

their son. She says she could never have imagined the intensity of the pain. Twelve months on, the pain had not eased one little bit. From an early age Michael had struggled with a chemical imbalance, which in his teens led to mental illness. This became so acute that eventually Michael took his own life.

A particular concern for his family was that Michael should be not only happy in the afterlife but whole in every sense. A series of extraordinary events took place at this point. Firstly Michael's doctor, who had treated him for years, began to have vivid dreams of Michael. Steve, Michael's younger brother, also began to have dreams in which many of the questions they had been asking themselves appeared to be being answered. Judy had prayed long and hard that her son was now at peace, and indications in these dreams seem to point to this being the case. One incredible event then took place that left Judy and her family in no doubt whatsoever that Michael was at peace and happy.

It was very early on a bright summer morning that Steve awoke. He drifted up from sleep slowly and sat up in bed. Rubbing his eyes, he saw to his incredulity his bedroom door slowly open. This happened in a controlled manner and completely unaided. Michael's room was across the hall, and the door of that room was also opened wide. Sitting on the bed was Michael. This was certainly no dream. Steve had had enough dreams of Michael recently to know the difference immediately. Perhaps those dreams had all been to prepare him for this experience.

Michael was dressed all in white and was glowing. Steve describes it as though he was lit from inside by a lamp. His face was pale and smooth, and his features were not as clearly defined as Steve remembered. Staring with fascination and deep intensity so as not to miss any details, Steve was transfixed.

When Steve had come to terms with the sight of his brother, Michael spoke. Softly he said, 'I am here to answer your questions and clarify your dreams.' He went on, 'You may ask anything you wish from me.' Steve remained calm, though feeling excited, and asked many questions. The answers elated and astonished him. Michael tried to explain how different earth and heaven were. Describing the vastness of heaven he said, 'By comparison you could fit the earth on a pinhead.' Music had always been a close bond between the brothers. Both had played guitars together for hours. Michael told his brother that music was now so fantastic in the other world that he could never begin to describe it. You would never hear anything remotely like it on earth, he added.

It was then that Steve asked the question everyone wanted an answer to. Was Michael well and at peace? The reply was emphatic: he was in a perfect state of mind, all illness completely gone. The peace was wonderful and a complete release. With this answered, Michael was gone, and Steve was left so elated that he could scarcely contain his joy.

Leaping out of bed, he rushed into Judy's room trying to tell her everything at once and no doubt not making much sense at first. Pulling his mother from the bedroom, he led her down the hall to Michael's room and to the exact spot where his brother had been. He had spoken to Steve with such calmness and clarity that they could only marvel and rejoice, remembering the dreadful state he had been in. Judy was elated as Steve struggled to communicate how happy his brother was. Finally he said, 'He is happy beyond anything we can feel on earth.' He had come to the conclusion that Michael had become a higher being, perhaps even an angel. His weak, sick brother was no more, having become strong, intelligent and free from all suffering. Steve could not emphasise enough that he was wide awake during this wonderful time, and there was absolutely no possibility that he had been dreaming.

Even though Michael had gone from the room, Steve and his mother could still feel his presence. All sense of guilt had gone. They now knew for certain that Michael loved them, and that he had, as Judy put it, given them 'soul growth'.

Maeve's story took place in the 1940s when tremendous changes were occurring in Britain. The Second World War was finally over, and the enormous task of rebuilding was underway. Manchester had its share of rebuilding and associated problems, and everyone was trying to get back to normal. The practical problems were compounded, however, by waves of childhood ailments. Gastroenteritis had reached almost epidemic proportions, and children were succumbing daily to it. Osteomyelitis was another problem at this time, when penicillin was only just becoming available.

Maeve thinks she was approximately four years of age at the time. Her family were soon touched by the tragedy of gastroenteritis like so many others around them. Maeve's little sister, only thirteen months old, was taken into hospital suffering from this distressing complaint and soon died. The whole family was devastated, and Maeve's mother was quite beside herself when suddenly Maeve too became seriously ill with measles. The doctor advised that she should go to hospital, but her mother would on no account allow her to go having only just lost one child in hospital. She nursed her herself, and would virtually not let her out of her sight.

Scarcely able to comprehend the events surrounding her, Maeve nevertheless recalls this time vividly. For comfort, warmth and convenience Maeve's bed was brought downstairs and erected in the living room. A large coal fire flickered in the hearth, and soon she was well enough to sit up in bed. It was at this point that for the first time Maeve noticed a large box in the corner of the room, placed on stilts. It was in those days the custom to bring the deceased into the house to await the day of the funeral. Maeve had no understanding of this or of what the large box contained, but she was told to try and remain quiet. She was comfortable and happy enough except at night, since she usually shared a room with her older sister. She requested a small bedside lamp which along with the glow from the fire would prevent the room from becoming too dark. This was arranged, and that night she felt considerably happier.

Fascinated by the coal fire, Maeve sat up in bed watching the glow of the embers and feeling warm and much better. Suddenly, to her surprise, she saw only a few feet away her little sister floating. She was close to ceiling height and dressed in a long white gown, and Maeve is certain she had wings because they moved as she hovered above her. It was then she asked Maeve, 'Do you want to come to heaven with me?' 'No,' answered Maeve, and at once the tiny angel faded away.

The incident is etched on Maeve's mind, and several factors puzzle her. How had her sister communicated, since at the time of her death she had not been able to speak? Maybe it was through transference, for Maeve is certain that this was not a dream, so clear is the memory. The coffin was taken away, and Maeve fully recovered. The events of that night will stay with Maeve forever, and she is more than certain that children who lose their lives go straight to heaven and become angels.

When a child dies, an angel comes down from heaven, takes the child in its arms and spreading out its large white wings visits all the places that had been particularly dear to the child. From the best loved place the angel gathers a handful of flowers, flying up again to heaven with them. Here they bloom more beautiful than on earth, but the flower which is most loved receives a voice so that it can join the song of the chorus of bliss.

HANS CHRISTIAN ANDERSEN

A trip to the park was the highlight of Nancy's week. In the summer Nancy's mother would often take sandwiches and fruit and they would have a picnic on the grass. Recently these trips had been tinged with sadness, for Nancy's friend Fiona had died that spring, and it did not seem quite the same without her. So many hours had been spent together in the park, and the little girl's infectious giggle was sorely missed. No-one could have guessed that the birthday party they had held for Fiona in the park only a few months ago would be her last.

It was going to be a hot day, so Nancy's mother said they would have a picnic in the park. She packed some of Nancy's favourite treats, and despite everything they walked happily to the park. After lunch Nancy decided to go to the area where the swings were, which was deserted. Sitting on her chosen swing, Nancy listlessly swung to and fro. Maybe she would like a good push, her mother reasoned. Putting down the book she had been reading, she stood up, intending to go across to her daughter. The sound of laughter made her look sharply towards the swing. Nancy was jumping off and running towards her in a state of some excitement.

With shining eyes, Nancy declared that everything would be all right now, for Fiona had come back from heaven. Apparently as she had been swinging sadly on her swing, she had been thinking about Fiona and wishing she could be there. Then the little girl's distinctive laugh had made Nancy turn round. A little distance behind her was Fiona! She was wearing a long white dress, and her hair was all sparkly. 'She must have come back, Mummy.'

Nancy's mother told her to sit down on the grass, and she then told her very gently what she thought had happened. She said that she too had heard the little girl's laughter, but she could not see her. She had not returned from heaven, but had been aware that Nancy was unhappy and had come back in the form of an angel to tell her that she was very happy and wanted her little friend to be happy also. Nancy perked up at that idea, and said Fiona must have found a wonderful park in heaven.

On the face of it our next story is one of heart-break, but when Diane got in touch with me her message was clearly that eventually a rainbow follows the storm. Hope is the key she offers to others in a similar situation. She feels that the telling of her story will inspire others to hold on, and I believe she is right.

When Diane lost her three-day-old son Darren, she felt a dramatic change in her life would help her to overcome the grief. It was decided that they should move house, so that a new area and new people might help them face the future more positively. The move did seem to help, and before too much time had elapsed Diane found herself pregnant again. Diane was full of optimism, and the pregnancy went smoothly. At last the day arrived, and Diane held in her arms a beautiful, healthy little girl.

The baby was christened Elaine, but at only three months old problems arose for her. Her initial good health started to deteriorate, and she was constantly sickly. Doctors assured Diane that all would eventually be well, but Diane had a terrible feeling inside that this would not be the case. All her instincts told her that this was more than an infant feeding problem.

One day Elaine was so poorly that an ambulance was

called, and the hospital decided to keep her as an inpatient to try and find out once and for all what the problem might be. Confusingly, all the tests proved negative. This only served to worry Diane and her husband more than ever. A pattern began of sending the child home, the child deteriorating, her returning to hospital, and yet more tests which always proved negative. It was like living in a nightmare. Each bout of illness left her weaker than before, and eventually the hospital admitted her for a very long stay to ensure everything possible would be investigated. This was intended to last for two months, but eventually it was discovered that Elaine had a very rare condition called orithine trancaromylase deficiency (ODT). This was to be treated by a special diet, and would mean a long road back to full recovery. At last a ray of hope!

Years went by, and Elaine started school. It was discovered there that she was wise beyond her years. She was a loving, kind girl, loved by everyone. Shortly after starting secondary school, Elaine became seriously ill again. All through her school life there had been long periods when she could not attend school, and had to pay numerous visits to the hospital. This time, however, it was clear a long stay was ahead, which was particularly depressing as she had a birthday approaching. The hospital staff produced a birthday cake, and they all sang to Elaine trying to make her day special. All the time doctors and nurses were telling Diane not to worry, but the icy cold feeling inside would not go away.

Finally, one beautiful summer's day, Elaine had dete-
riorated yet again and, whilst she slept, Diane slipped
out into the grounds of the hospital for some much
needed fresh air and to be alone for a while. Looking
up at the window of her daughter's room she saw her
pale face appear at the window. At once she rushed
back to be with her. 'Who was the lady with you on the
grass?' Elaine asked. 'I was alone, darling,' her mother
replied. 'I saw her very clearly, Mummy, she said. 'She
was wearing a beautifully coloured dress full of
flowers.' Elaine explained that she had just woken from
a lovely dream. She had been in a very special place
where she was no longer sick and did not have to take
any medicine or pills, and she was very happy there. 'I
want to go back there, Mummy,' she said. 'It was
beautiful. I want to die.'

Diane was stunned to hear her daughter say these
things, and stared in disbelief. All she could do to cope
was to change the subject completely. Soon after this,
Elaine grew very weary and leaning back in her pillows
looked very frail. She opened her eyes and said, 'I love
you, Mummy' and these proved to be her last words.
The life-support machine was switched off, and Diane
felt the very depth of despair.

One of the consequences of all this heartache and
stress was the break-up of Diane's marriage and Diane
then felt completely alone.

The years have rolled by. Diane in time married
again and is extremely happy in her marriage. Over the

years she has had angelic communication from both her children, and she says they are now definitely free from sickness and pain and extremely happy. She feels without a shadow of doubt that they will all be reunited one day in the spiritual world. She adds that she is living proof that even the depths of despair can be overcome, and there truly is light at the end of the tunnel.

Silently one by one, in the infinite meadows of heaven blossom the lovely stars, the forget-me-nots of angels.
HENRY WORDSWORTH LONGFELLOW

Harry was a thoroughly nice, kind, decent man, much loved by family and friends. So his daughter-in-law said, and it was she who told me this amazing story. Carol instantly liked Harry from the first moment they met. In time she grew to love him as a father, and Harry loved her along with his son and grandchildren. The children were aware that they had a very special grandfather. He would tell Carol she was the daughter he had always wanted, and he helped cement together a very happy extended family.

One night Harry began to feel unwell. A pain in his chest made him go to bed early, but he decided a good night's sleep was all he needed to get him back to normal. During the night Harry died. The entire family was devastated, but for Carol there was an extra pain. The birth of her third child was imminent, and she had so wanted Harry to see his new grandchild. More distressing still was that Carol gave birth during the time of Harry's funeral. Unable to attend, she felt keenly that she had been unable to say goodbye. Gazing down at her new-born son, she felt joy and grief in equal measures.

Several days elapsed, and Carol carried on the normal care of her new-born son in a bit of a daze. He was a good baby, and people remarked that he looked a little like Harry. How Carol wished he had seen him. Sleep would not come for her this particular night, even though the baby was sleeping soundly. Carol was sitting up in bed awaiting her husband who was unavoidably late. The bedside clock showed the time as just after midnight, and she was wide awake, looking forward to her husband getting home.

Presently she became aware of something strange happening in the room; there was a definite feeling of a presence in the altered atmosphere. At the foot of the bed a glow started to build until it became a bright light. Carol stared transfixed as slowly emerging from the light came the figure of Harry. He smiled as he spoke. He told her that he had come to see the new baby and to say goodbye, although she must not forget that he would never be far away.

Slowly the vision faded, until the room was once more in darkness save for a tiny lamp.

Carol had not felt a trace of fear, only calmness and a tremendous sense of comfort. She looked at her sleeping new-born son and for the first time she could distinctly see the likeness to his grandfather. A noise from the next room startled her; both her daughters were crying. Quickly slipping out of bed, she rushed to the girls bedroom. 'Whatever is the matter?' she asked. Her elder daughter, still a toddler but bright and articulate, said, 'Grandpa just said goodbye. Where has he gone?' Gathering her little girls in her arms, Carol told them that he would never be far away and would always watch over them. The fact was that he had gone to be an angel in heaven.

North Wales is an area of great natural beauty. Jennifer and Clare were very excited as they had been to Wales several times before, and loved all it had to offer. Like all children they thought the beach essential, and spent many hours paddling in rock pools and building sand castles. This year they were staying in a familiar little seaside town, and renting a lovely seaside cottage.

Early one evening after spending the whole day on the beach, the family arrived back at the cottage to prepare the evening meal. The girls were still full of energy, running in and out of the house and through the garden, chasing each other and squealing with delight. Climbing up to the breakfast bar, the girls were still giddy, so their mother asked them to calm down and eat their evening meal a little less noisily. At that moment Jennifer reached across to give Clare a mischievous poke in the ribs. What happened next changed their lives for ever. Jennifer overturned her stool losing her balance, and fell backwards with great force into the patio doors. Her parents saw it all happen as if in slow motion, horrified but helpless to prevent the impact.

To everyone's disbelief Jennifer was declared dead on arrival at the hospital. Her neck had been broken in the fall, since she had hit the doors with great force and at a dangerous angle. A happy family holiday had turned into a nightmare in one split second. Clare was in such a state of despair that no-one knew how to console her. She missed her sister very much, and most nights would cry herself to sleep. The one thing that worried Clare above all others was where Jennifer was and if she felt pain. She talked incessantly about heaven and wanted to know what it was like. Was Jennifer there, and was she lonely without them?

Several months went by, and the situation was no easier. Clare would lie awake fretting. Soon it would be the day of Jennifer's birthday, and everyone was dreading it. At nine years old she was old enough to understand the pain of loss, but too young to be able to cope with it.

Sitting up in bed with the sheet pulled up to her

chin, she switched on the bedside light to try and read a book, but she had no heart for it. Suddenly another light appeared at the foot of her bed, and in the centre of this light she saw Jennifer. She had on a dress of pure white, and light appeared to dance around her head. She was smiling the broad, happy smile Clare remembered so well. She raised a hand towards Clare as if in greeting, and then she was gone as quickly as she had appeared. The only light was now from the little bedside lamp, and the room seemed very dark. Clare's worst fear and greatest nagging question had been dealt with. Her sister had wanted her to know she was happy and perfectly all right, and there was no need for Clare to worry about her.

Clare has never forgotten her sister of course, and would never want to. She misses her still, almost ten years later. Inside, however, is a warm glow of knowledge emanating from the assurance that she has a little sister among the angels.

Jason considered owning a motorbike to be the pinnacle of happiness and could not wait until he was old enough to own one. Close friends of the family had an eighteen-year-old son, Jeremy, who would ride his large shiny bike past Jason's house. Whenever Jason was in earshot, Jason would plead with him to let him ride on the pillion.

At last, after months of pleading, Jeremy finally agreed that he would take Jason for a very short ride. This, he reasoned, might at least keep him quiet for a little time. He handed him a helmet and said it would be no more than a trip around the block. Jason was beside himself with excitement as he climbed on the huge shiny bike.

It is uncertain just what sequence of events took place, but one thing is clear. They found themselves unable to avoid hitting a car in front of them, which in turn had ploughed into the car in front. Inevitably traffic behind hit them, and there was a pile-up of crashed vehicles.

The boys were taken to hospital and then surgery, and it became clear that Jason's injuries were very serious indeed. Despite intensive surgery and life-support systems, Jason only lived for a day after surgery. He never regained consciousness. His parents could hardly believe the events of the past twenty-four hours, and sat by their son's bedside in deep distress.

A family friend happened to be a nurse at the hospital and on duty at this tragic time. It was a help to know a close friend had been there, looking after Jason and comforting them. This friend had stayed with them in Jason's room, and used all her professional skills.

The parents wished to be alone for a while with Jason, so their friend left. As she closed the door behind her, she noticed a man across the corridor struggling with a pair of crutches. She went across to his bedside to help him stand straight on his crutches. 'Has the young boy died?' he asked. With a surprised look she answered, 'Yes,' wondering how he knew since the door to Jason's room had been closed at all times. 'A few minutes ago I saw an angel standing in the corridor outside the room,' he said. 'It was only for a split second, but I was convinced he had taken the young boy with him.'

In the stories of this chapter we have seen the courage of parents facing the loss of a much loved child. I have been approached by many parents asking me to include their particular story in the hope that it would help and comfort others. I sincerely hope so too. Many of the accounts are harrowing, and the pain these people face is hard to imagine, but the longing to help others shines through.

This is certainly true of Lisa, who firmly believes that children have an inherent link with angels and the spiritual world. She feels this is the only explanation for the events surrounding the death of her young son.

Lisa's son was suffering from leukaemia and losing the battle. He grew very weak, and they all knew the end was not too far away. He became so weak that speech was impossible, and Lisa was extremely distressed. The family was not religious and had never expressed any views on the afterlife. With startling suddenness, her son opened his eyes and said that he could quite distinctly see two angels standing at the foot of his bed. She is sure no-one had ever mentioned angels, and there was certainly no literature around the house on the subject. Everyone was astonished.

The statement her son made as he lay dying has been the most wonderful comfort to Lisa. She believes it was deeply significant that he could find the strength to talk to them and tell them that wonderful things were happening for him. She thought it was proof positive that he would be cared for and happy in another life.

For a child to grasp what happens when someone dies is clearly very difficult. Some children, however, seem to have everything worked out very well. I would like to end this chapter with an amusing but inspiring story. During a children's angel workshop I chatted to Thomas. He was five years old, and his father had died when he was only a baby. He sat at the table listening to other children talk about angels, and then spoke up with great authority. 'Here is what happens,' he said. 'First of all you are poorly, then you are very poorly indeed, and then you die. It is then that you have go into a big box called a coffin, but it's all right because that's when the angels come. The angels' special job is to take you to heaven, and there you will be very happy.' With that cleared up for everyone, he went back to his drawing. I thought again as I had during several children's workshops: where does all their wisdom come from? Thank you, Thomas Lloyd, for your very valuable input.

Thomas has remarkable insight, but sometimes these matters can confuse. One child attending a memorial service for a classmate, asked his teacher why had she told him that his little friend was in heaven. The teacher answered the child positively, saying that the classmate was now an angel. 'Why is she standing behind the candles then?' he asked. The child's forthright and matter-of-fact question brought great comfort to the grieving mother.

I recall being told about a young boy sent upstairs to tell his grandfather that lunch was about to be served. The boy came down again and said, 'Grandpa is talking to the angels,' totally at ease with the scene. His parents discovered that the grandfather was dead in his chair. How wonderful to be so accepting and unafraid in these circumstances.

7

Mystery Angels

In recent years there have been an increasing number of television programmes devoted to mysteries. It seems we are fascinated by things that cannot be explained, such as stories of extraterrestrial activity, crop circles and earth mysteries. Angels certainly have a great air of mystery attached to them. Encounters that do not appear to have a reason have mystified the people concerned. People not in immediate danger, seriously ill or depressed are delighted but confused as to why the event took place.

The most extraordinary event can arise out of the most mundane situation. Rosemary, for instance, believed it to be a very ordinary day as she sat in her garden one summer. Fudge bounded across the lawn in only a few strides. He was growing larger by the day and still only a puppy. Fudge was most definitely a kind of therapy; his presence was very soothing, and she was forced to take some exercise at least once a day. The fresh air and brisk walk always lifted her spirits considerably. Several years had elapsed since the death of her young daughter at six months old. Rosemary and her husband had hoped that in time they might become parents again, but so far this had not happened.

The day was wonderful, and Rosemary made a pot of tea and sat down at the garden table. Fudge settled at her feet, and she decided that when the evening came and with it cooler air she would take him for a very long walk. Suddenly, from the bottom of the garden, there was a rustle in the flower bushes. Fudge sat upright and pricked up his ears. Slowly and purposefully a little girl stepped out into the sunshine and full view. She had a halo of blonde curls and a broad smile directed straight at Rosemary.

Taken by surprise, Rosemary took a second or so to respond. 'Hello, where did you come from?' she asked. There was no reply. Confused, Rosemary approached the child. 'Are you lost?' she asked, bending low towards the child. The child had a certain mesmerising quality, but still she did not answer. Leaning forward, the little girl kissed Rosemary on the cheek, and then walked on past the house and down the side path leading to the front gate.

With a sensation of being released from a spell and suddenly galvanised into action, Rosemary ran down the side path to catch up with the child. She was nowhere to be seen, even though only seconds had elapsed. The garden, the quiet road – all empty. The front garden path was quite long, and to the side of the house was an empty flat field. She could not have been in that field without being seen. Several metres of lawn separated their front garden from the house next door, so again she would have been seen clearly had she walked in that direction.

Some time later, climbing the stairs in her house, Rosemary found herself wandering into the nursery. Gazing out across the lawn, she thought again of her lovely baby. The question came into her head like a bolt from the blue: how old would her child have been now? She placed a hand on her cheek where the little girl had kissed it. I wonder, thought Rosemary, I wonder . . .

> *We trust in plumed procession*
> *for such the angels go*
> *Rank after rank, with even feet*
> *and uniforms of snow.*
> EMILY DICKINSON

Ian had had a scientific education, but was still on a spiritual journey. He was interested in learning about all aspects of spirituality, and his spiritual horizons were expanding.

It was late one night, and he was soundly asleep one

minute and then wide awake the next with no idea why or how he had suddenly been roused from sleep. Sitting up in bed, he was suddenly aware of a presence in the room, even though the bedroom door was firmly shut. In front of the door there then appeared a figure, glowing and golden, radiating light. Although he knew for certain he was wide awake, to make sure he turned away and touched the bedroom wall. It was solid and real, and no dream. As he looked again towards the door, the figure was still there in full view and so clear that every detail is etched in Ian's memory. It remained for some considerable time, and did not vanish in seconds like so many accounts relate. The figure was physically very beautiful and dressed in a long glowing robe which had the appearance of being composed of pure energy. It was male and very tall.

There is no question in Ian's mind that this was real. It was not a dream and certainly not a projection of his own imagination. Eventually the figure gave Ian the most wonderful smile before slowly vanishing. Ian had the distinct impression that he was checking on his spiritual progress and journey.

Ian had often reflected on the inner spiritual ability, which he now sees as corresponding to Swedenborg's description of the angel within. He found himself some time later in a position to use this inner angel. Sitting in a comfortable armchair, he was contentedly reading and feeling quite relaxed. The peace was soon disturbed, however, by the insistent crying of a baby on the other side of the wall. This baby was obviously in the flat next door and clearly distressed. The crying persisted, and no-one appeared to be attending to the child. The decibel level and the distress increased, and it was then that with an almost reflex action Ian stretched out his arm towards the wall.

He projected a flow of golden light and energy towards the infant, spontaneously and without prior thought. Instantly the baby stopped crying and became peaceful. How often do we read about the golden light radiating peace and love accompanying an angel? It is clearly a quality within us all. We can all try harder to reach out and project love through our own particular walls.

Occasionally a story reaches me where the child visited by an angel can think of no obvious reason at all why it should do so. In the case of Natasha I can only think that the child was so happy and full of joy that the angels wanted to join in! Natasha was the youngest of a family of four children, loved by all her siblings and parents. They were a well-off family, and the home was large and well appointed. Every child had a room of his or her own, and Natasha loved her spacious bedroom in the large

Victorian house. Of all her toys Natasha loved her magnificent dolls' house the most, and would spend hours in her room absorbed in the make-believe world it promoted. When she had extra money she would often go and buy tiny furniture for the dolls' house.

Autumn was approaching, and the evenings were darkening rapidly. It was a Saturday and the whole family had decided to go to a new shopping mall not too far away. They were to have lunch there, and everyone looked forward with pleasure to the proposed trip. Natasha bought a couple of items for her dolls' house and was very happy.

At supper time they all chatted happily about the new shopping mall. Before bedtime Natasha decided she would go upstairs a little early in order to place the new items of furniture in her house before it was time to go to sleep. Gazing around her bedroom she smiled to herself with delight at the memory of the lovely day. She felt cosy, loved and very fortunate.

The next moment she was surprised when without warning the room was suddenly filled with glowing spheres of light slightly bigger than a tennis ball. Natasha described them as appearing to be lit from inside with a brilliant light radiating in all directions as they whirled through the air. The feeling they gave her was one of love and happiness, which complemented her own feelings exactly. The room had its heavy curtains drawn, and Natasha is certain the lights could not have been reflections from an outside source. They were, she insists, far more than just spheres of light; they positively glowed and filled her with joy.

As an adult Natasha has often tried to explain the events of that night. She has never experienced anything similar since. She has concluded that the lights were some sort of angelic manifestation. It was as if they were sharing in her happiness and rejoicing in the fact that one so young could fully appreciate all she had. The idea of angels playing with a child and giving and receiving love is very beautiful.

All God's angels come to us disguised.
JAMES RUSSELL LOWELL

There is no such thing as a 'normal' angel story; they are innately special and unique to the person involved. Certain characteristics or common denominators can be detected, but each one has its own heavenly insight. The following story, however, is particularly unusual. On the surface the story is about a cheerful little boy with a cheeky smile, but it also has a mystical dimension.

The story happened in India in 1910, where Fozia's grandfather grew up. It was the most extraordinary event in her grandfather's childhood, and is etched on his memory. He attended a religious school which was quite strict, and encouraged the boys to study hard. Fozia's grandfather was a diligent student and was most inspired by his learned 'ustad' or teacher, a very learned, wise and discreet old man. One day a new boy arrived at the school, and everyone was intrigued by him. He was a mystery; no-one was quite sure where he had come from or who his family was. The wise ustad said nothing to the other boys, and told them simply to get on with their work and not to be intrusive.

No matter how much they questioned him, the new boy was very vague in his answers about his background, and would cleverly field any penetrating questions. In all other respects he appeared normal. He was cheerful and popular except for the fact that he won all physical games hands down with an apparent ease that irritated his classmates. It was suspected by many at the school that the old ustad knew a great deal more about the boy than he let on, but he always kept his counsel. The boy was treated exactly the same as anyone else, firmly but fairly.

One day a group of boys were walking outside the school and were passing a house under construction. The workmen were struggling to lift a large heavy wooden beam into place. Curiosity rooted the boys to the spot, as they wondered how on earth they would manage this monster of a beam. More men were called to help, but time after time they were defeated. After resting for a moment, several men decided to have one more try, but to no avail. They shook their heads in despair.

At this moment the new boy stepped forward, and whilst everyone stared open-mouthed he lifted the enormous beam single-handed, and placed it into position as if lifting a feather. He had, in short, performed the impossible. Fozia's grandfather ran like the wind back to school to tell the ustad what had happened. He was told to be discreet and not to broadcast the incident, as people would not understand.

When the boys were gathered together, the ustad spoke to them. They could scarcely believe their ears when this wise old man told them that this child was an angel sent to earth in human form to help and guide wherever he was needed.

The amazing child moved on as quickly as he had come, mysteriously telling no-one where he was going and leaving no address or any other trace. Fozia's grandfather told the story so often that it was clear that many years later he was still puzzled about the boy and the dramatic events of that day so long ago. India is truly a land of mystery.

Dusk was falling on the village of Tythegston in Glamorgan, Wales, as Wendy set out on an errand. The village was too small to have a shop, but Mr Durston kept a store of essential things in his own house and would sell them from there. It was to his house that Wendy was sent.

At the age of eight Wendy was a sensitive and religious girl, who attended the village church. It was a very pleasing shape, and she enjoyed attending and singing the hymns. The light was beginning to fade as she passed the old church, but she noticed a faint flickering in the church window. The window was a large arched one and faced the lane. Mrs Maggie Mathews took care of the church, and Wendy assumed that she was inside busy with some task. Drawing level with the window, Wendy looked up, totally unprepared for the sight that met her. In silhouette against the lighted window was a huge angel. It reminded her of the Renaissance paintings she had seen. Long heavy wings reached from the top of the figure to the toes. Standing still as a statue, she was spellbound, as she watched the wings move and settle in the way a bird's would. There was a bright glow surrounding the angel, whilst in the background the more gentle light continued to flicker, producing an effect similar to a gas or oil lamp.

Wanting others to see this spectacular sight, she suddenly found her feet and ran as fast as she could to Mr Durston's house, a short distance away. Knocking urgently on his door, she exclaimed with a sharp intake of breath that there was an angel in the church. The kindly gentleman smiled in bemusement and said, 'It must be Mrs Mathews, dear.' He did, though, accompany her to the church as quickly as possible. Alas, the church was now in total darkness, and Wendy could have cried with disappointment. They elicited, however, that Mrs Mathews had not been anywhere near the church that evening, and no-one else had. Wendy knew that she had not been mistaken, and had definitely seen an angel in the church window.

Now an adult, she visits the village from time to time. It has changed little and is still unspoilt and beautiful. She regards herself as very fortunate indeed to have seen such a sight. Gazing up at the window on her infrequent visits, she always feels a 'tingle in the spine' as the memory of that summer evening floods back.

Many children, it would seem, momentarily glimpse an angel. Like Wendy, they will not be in need of rescue or seriously ill, but they do grow with a strong sense of the spiritual world.

On reflection, a graveyard might be a likely place to see an angel and several stories have reached me about such a location. Children, accompanying mothers placing flowers on a grave, have wandered off and seen angels. One young girl reports seeing two huge, transparent angels, which she insists were definitely not the stone carvings. Often the vision lasts for just a second, and frequently the adults involved dismiss the incident as mere fantasy.

Angelic intervention, however, is often a clear warning and maybe comes in guises we least expect. Every mother will tell you how impossible it is to keep her children within sight twenty-four hours a day. No matter how careful and diligent a mother you are, there will always be the odd occasion when you are distracted and a child will face danger.

In the summer of 1998 Pam and her children were outdoors enjoying the sunshine. Alex was two-and-a-half years old and his sister Ebony only one. Their older sister, Alycia, was at playgroup, so Pam thought they could spend the morning playing in the garden in the sunshine. The house had a long garden; at the top was a flagged patio and at the bottom a large sandpit. The patio was attached to a conservatory, which led to the kitchen. Shortly after lunch Pam went indoors to wash the dishes, leaving the children on the patio area playing.

Staring into the soapy water, Pam was suddenly startled by a strong odour, which seemed to literally hit her in the face. The smell reminded Pam of dirt or earth, as if someone had thrown dirt into her face. It was a most unusual occurence, and startled Pam into looking up from the kitchen sink.

Through the window she saw that the children had moved from the patio area to the bottom of the garden and were in the sandpit. Alex was throwing sand into the baby's face. Going cold at the thought of the damage to eyes, nose and mouth this could cause, Pam rushed outside and rescued Ebony. It was only after the incident, when Ebony was washed clean of sand, that Pam realised what a clear warning she had received. She believes she was alerted by a guardian angel to prevent a potentially dangerous incident.

Velvet was a handsome, black, cocker spaniel, much loved by the Grindall family in general and Ray in particular. His outstanding characteristic was fearlessness; he would happily engage in combat with dogs twice his size and quite ferocious.

One evening when Ray was in his early teens, he sat by the fire with a book in the company of his father. They were keeping a respectful silence because Ray's grandmother who lived with the family was dangerously ill. Upstairs Ray's mother was sitting by the old lady's bedside and Velvet lay at the side of the bed, aware that all was not normal. Ray's grandmother had lived with them for three years, since the death of her much loved husband, George. He had been missed very much, especially by his wife.

Slipping into a coma, Ray's grandmother seemed to be fading. Her daughter held her hand in concern, and Velvet watched with large patient eyes. Suddenly Ray and his father were startled by the noise of Velvet thudding down the stairs, whimpering and howling intermittently. They were astonished to see Velvet hurl himself into the room visibly shaking and with the hair on his back standing on end.

They rushed upstairs to the bedroom to try and see what the matter could be. Calmly, Ray's mother related the events of the past few minutes. Grandma had sunk deeper into a coma and was not responding to her daughter at all. Without warning, however, she suddenly woke, lifted her head from the pillow and stared at a point in the corner of the room. Showing no sign of frailty at this moment, she broke out into the most brilliant smile and said, 'Hello, George,' before sinking back and dying peacefully. Simultaneously Velvet had jumped up, stared at the very same spot in the room, let out a yelp of fright, backed out of the room with his hair on end, and hurled himself down the stairs yelping.

Ray is quite certain that his grandfather had appeared in angel form to take his grandmother to heaven, and that Velvet had seen him too. He adds that nothing of this world would ever frighten that fearless dog.

Picture the scene of a school Nativity play with dozens of infants dressed in angel costumes. Paul was six years old, and although he did not have a speaking part in this extravaganza he was enjoying taking part. Swept along the corridor to the stage, he tumbled out and found his place right at the front of the stage where he had to sit throughout. He was quite happy with this arrangement, because he could see all the action and everyone coming and going.

A tall woman entered the stage from the corridor. She carried a small baby in her arms and was accompanied by a little girl of about ten years of age. They wore long white dresses and walked slowly to the back of the stage where the woman sat on a chair. The girl knelt beside her and placed her hands together, appearing to pray.

Paul stared in fascination, since he had never seen them before. He was intrigued by the fact that they had bare feet. The most captivating feature, however, was the huge beautiful pair of wings the woman had. Paul can remember vividly being able to see each feather clearly. The contrast with the children's cellophane and sellotaped wings was dramatic. Paul says it is a sight he will never forget.

Paul nudged the boy sitting next to him and pointed the little trio out to him. The boy gave a vague shrug and appeared to be totally uninterested. Paul slowly realised that no-one could see these figures. It was years later that he realised that these figures were not actors in the entertainment but real angels – and he was the only person to have seen them.

Children and Angels

ANGEL WINGS

The children giggle as they straggle across a makeshift stage
Some shy, some uncertain, some keen to figure in the play
Besides the homespun stable, the splendour of kings
What fascinates me most are the angels wings
How best to represent this unearthly elegance
Wire threaded tinsel, foil on cardboard or nets of gossamer
*   pretence?*
Should they be heart shaped, modest as infants
Or broad and sweeping as those of stone on Faxman's tombs?
Children have their spilling innocence to give them wings
But how do ours grow to lofty fulfilment in our being?
Glorious dreams need nurture, but repay the cradling
Of our heart's desire, so that each angel finds a place where
*   wings*
Touch others and give unvaunted uplifting power with
*   surprise*
At how they may bless these earthly lives.

DAVID LOMAX

Mirrors have always held a great fascination. For Rita, one Sunday afternoon, a glance into a mirror brought more than the reflection she had expected. About to leave home and visit friends, she was ready for a well earned break from home decorating. She had worked hard on her house, filling it with bright, warm colours to replace the dark interior. The crowning glory was the large antique mirror she had bought for the hall. It had cost a great deal more than she had intended, but it looked beautiful and reflected the light exactly as she wanted.

Picking up her gloves and handbag, she had a last look in the mirror to check her hair. Raising a hair-brush halfway to her head, Rita froze in mid-action. Staring into her eyes from behind her shoulder was a little girl. Rita knew for certain she was alone in the house and the mirror faced a blank wall. The hall had only one door and that was at the far end away from the mirror. The girl was smiling at Rita through the mirror and her face positively radiated light. She also seemed to be surrounded by a bright glow.

Once the shock had worn off, Rita found this vision lovely and captivating, and she could scarcely move. Eventually spurred into action, she twisted around quickly, but there was nothing behind her – no trace of the little girl. Glancing back into the mirror she saw only her own reflection. Thinking about that day, she realised that it been the first time had looked into the mirror. She lives alone and feels now that this little child was a guardian angel.

E veryone must be familiar with the phenomenon of hearing some fascinating fact for the first time and then in a short space of time coming across it again in some form or other. It happened to me while researching this book. I heard an angel story unlike any I had ever heard before, and whilst I was pondering on it another one of startling similarity came to my notice. Three thousand miles separate the children involved, so I find it even more remarkable.

The first account comes from Philadelphia, USA, and involves a young girl sitting by a swimming pool momentarily alone. On the other side of the pool a man appeared dressed in a white suit and standing next to a poolside table. As she watched, the man slowly faded away. The child got up from her chair and walked around the pool to the spot where he had stood. To her astonishment there was a note on the table warning her not to go into the pool. On a second separate occasion the child again found a warning note, and this time it was signed with a name. Her family firmly believes the notes were left by her guardian angel.

The second story takes place in Cumbria, England, in the heart of the beautiful Lake District. Josh was ten years old and on holiday with his extended family. Josh and his cousins were passionate fishermen, and it was to be a fishing-orientated break.

The three cousins set out on their first day in the Lakes, carrying all their tackle and a bag full of sandwiches and drinks. The day grew very hot, and the boys thought the lake might be the perfect place to cool off. They had been warned, however, not to swim in the lakes, which are deceptively deep and always cold even in the hottest weather. Ignoring the warning, they decided to go ahead and have a swim. Removing their clothes and placing them in a pile beside the fishing gear, they headed towards the water's edge.

Just as they were about to take the plunge, something made Josh turn around. He saw a man standing beside their clothes dressed in a white suit. Before Josh's startled eyes, this man slowly faded away.

Letting out a yell of surprise, he ran towards their belongings, swiftly followed by his two cousins. There on top of the clothes was a note written on a large piece of paper which read: 'You must not go into the water.' The boys hurriedly dressed and ran back to the cottage. It was Josh's mother who told me that no-one could ever doubt their sincerity, since they were so shocked and had the note for all to see.

Sue grew up with a view of London's rooftops from her bedroom window. She found the view endlessly fascinating, and would sit by her window admiring the different levels and varying types of roof tiles. At night there was the extra bonus of seeing an uninterrupted view of the stars, and on bright moonlit nights all the rooftops were floodlit.

One particularly clear starry night is etched in Sue's memory forever. It was cold and clear, and the stars were very bright. Knowing that she would have a lovely view of the stars, she went to her favourite window-seat to look out. The most surprising thing ever to have happened to Sue then took place. There, directly in front of her window, standing on a flat rooftop in full view, was an angel!

Although only four years old at the time, every detail remains as fresh as if it were yesterday. The figure was immense, dressed in long, white, glistening robes. The wings almost defied description, they were so large, starting well above the head of the angel and reaching right down to the ground. Each feather was clearly defined. In the moonlight she could clearly see the face and described it as humanlike but with no defining male or female features.

Why, she now wonders, would a child so young see

154

an angel outside her bedroom window? There was no obvious danger, and the incident puzzled Sue for many years. As an adult, however, further spiritual experiences have occurred at difficult times in her life, and she feels that the angel prepared the way. She was able to 'open up' and receive such help without fear. Whatever the reason, it certainly was a night to remember.

> *Angels always appear in a bright light. They have to*
> *be able to see where they are going.*
>
> Lucy, 5

Jessica's older sister Rosie was howling with pain. She had rushed from the garden to chat with a friend on the footpath and had trodden on a piece of glass. Her foot was bleeding profusely, and her mother knew a trip to casualty would be necessary.

Casualty was full to bursting, and they realised they would have to endure a long wait. Time wore on, and no matter how many patients were attended to, the hall never seemed to get less full. Jessica started to wander around with boredom, and at that moment Rosie was asked to go into the treatment room. Picking up the baby and momentarily disctracted, Jessica's mother ushered Rosie in to see the doctor.

Seconds later, Jessica realised they had gone. She rushed down the corridor where she had seen others go as they left the main hall. The corridor was full of blue doors on either side, and there was no way of knowing which one her family had gone through. Pressing on down the busy corridor, she found herself turning left and then right, and then she was hopelessly lost.

She then noticed a door leading outside and thought maybe her mother and sisters had gone out to the car. Pushing the doors, she found herself in a huge car park. Wandering down endless rows of cars, she began to cry. There was no sign of her mother's car or her mother and sisters, and panic was rising inside her.

At that moment a tall woman stepped out from behind a row of cars, smiling, and took hold of Jessica's hand. Silently she led her through the door back inside the hospital. With absolute surety she went down the hospital corridors until they came to the one with all the blue doors. Stopping outside one, she pushed it open and there sitting on a chair with the baby in her lap was Jessica's mother. Rosie was on a table having her foot attended to, and Jessica rushed towards them with relief.

Jessica's mother asked where she had been, since there were people outside looking for her. 'I was lost and went outside by mistake,' Jessica answered, 'but the lady brought me back.' 'Which one?' her mother asked. 'The one who opened the door for me just now,' Jessica replied. 'You were alone when you came through that door,' her mother said.

Jessica insisted that she had been brought back by

the tall lady. As they left the treatment room, her mother asked a woman waiting outside on a chair if she had seen the little girl come down the corridor. 'Yes,' she answered, 'she came all the way down this long corridor and straight into the treatment room.' 'Did you see the lady with her?' she asked. 'The little girl was alone,' said the woman. 'I saw her go through the door by herself.'

'I think you must have a guardian angel,' her mother said, and Jessica could see she was not joking.

> *Angels come to earth to help people and then they disappear.*
> Kirsty, 10

The breakfast porridge was almost ready. Karen had given her daughter a tangerine to eat whilst waiting. Handing the fruit to her casually, she hoped she would eat it without question, since fruit was the only food Karen had difficulty getting her daughter to eat.

It was a rather strange sensation making breakfast in her mother's house. She could not believe that she would not come into the room, busy and cheerful. It was three years since her mother had died, and Karen's daughter Catherine had been born around the same time. She would never know her grandmother, and that was a great sadness for Karen. Lost in her own thoughts, Karen stirred the porridge only vaguely aware that Catherine was chatting away. She had decided that Catherine could perhaps see her aunt through the kitchen door and was talking to her. Turning to face her daughter, she saw the kitchen was still empty and that no-one was occupying the adjoining room. No-one else was out of bed, it appeared. Who, then, was Catherine talking to?

'I was talking to your mummy,' Catherine said. Taken aback, Karen asked where she had been. 'Up there,' said Catherine, pointing to a spot on the ceiling. 'She told me that I must eat my fruit because it was very good for me.' Karen was dumbfounded.

Soon it was bedtime for Catherine. She was tucked up in bed, and everyone in turn kissed her goodnight. She appeared to settle down happily enough. A short time later, Karen's father came downstairs and said to her 'Catherine is chatting away upstairs. I don't know what it's all about.'

Dashing up the stairs as quickly and quietly as she could, Karen stood behind the bedroom door. Sure enough, Catherine was chatting animatedly. Slowly Karen put her head around the door. Her daughter was staring up at the ceiling, smiling and talking away. Pushing the door open, Karen asked if she was all right. 'Yes,' came the reply. 'I was talking to your mummy again.' This time she added, 'She looked so pretty in her long pink dress with flowers in her hand.'

Stunned, Karen could scarcely take this in, because her mother had been buried in a long pink dress. She loved roses and always had some near. Entering the room at this point to see what was going on, Karen's sister remarked on the overpowering scent of roses. She too was astonished to find that there were no flowers of any kind in the room and the windows were firmly shut.

Catherine never saw her grandmother again. It was as if she had come to say goodbye from the angelic realms. But to this day, from time to time, the house is full of the scent of roses.

Three short stories reached me with an unusual common feature. No angels were seen, heard or felt, and yet each person is convinced the incidents were of an angelic nature.

Paula was sitting in the garden on a very hot day in summer reading a book. She had the house and garden to herself, and she was enjoying the peace. Like so many teenagers at this time of the year she was studying for her GCSE examinations. All sorts of little things distracted her – bees, the drone of an aeroplane – but mostly she was dwelling on the long summer break ahead.

Almost dozing, she was surprised to be suddenly blasted by very cold air – bizarre on such a hot day. It seemed to swirl around her before stopping just as quickly. She glanced around, but the garden was perfectly still, and the kitchen door was firmly closed. Where could such an icy cold blast have come from on a hot, still afternoon? Putting down her book, she decided to go indoors for a drink, and glancing at her watch noticed it was exactly three o'clock.

At five o'clock Paula gave up on study, and decided to go indoors and start the evening meal for her mother. Washing the salad, she heard the car pull up into the drive. Her mother came into the kitchen looking pale and upset. 'What's wrong?' her daughter asked. She had gone to Paula's grandmother's to have a chat and a cup of tea, only to find her dead in her garden chair. It was a terrible shock, and she could not yet accept it. Paula put her arms around her mother and said, 'Tell me all about it while I make a drink for you. Firstly, what time did it happen? 'Three o'clock,' her mother replied. For the second time that afternoon Paula went cold.

Peter was twelve when his father died. It was no surprise to anyone, for he had battled with cancer for almost two years. Although the family was relieved for him, they were also bereft. It took many months before Peter could come to terms with the fact that his father was no longer there.

Two years passed, and late one night Peter was sitting in the lounge reading a magazine. Once more he found himself thinking about his father and wishing he was still there with him. Behind his chair a cold draft wafted past, and felt almost like fingers on his neck. Peter did not look round to see where it had come from or ponder for a second about what it meant. 'No question about it,' he says, 'that was my father.'

Our third story on this theme is from Diane. She too was in her garden on a hot day when the air was very still. Suddenly, from nowhere a strong breeze shook the willow tree violently. This lasted for just a minute, and then everything was still again. That day her grandmother was attending the funeral of a relative. Diane's mother believes the gust of wind was the spirit of their relative on the way to heaven.

Children and Angels

Jean and her son David were about to embark on a complicated trip, which involved travelling down to London, then changing for a journey to East Anglia. Jean was nervous as she was unused to travel, and to add to the concern David had just recently been diagnosed as a diabetic. They had been invited to spend Easter with a group of friends, and they had been looking forward to it immensely. Jean decided that she would not let her anxiety spoil the holiday. Jean's father drove them to the station and helped them with their luggage. The first part was fairly straightforward, and they settled back into their seats until they came to Euston, London.

The bustle of the huge station brought a rising panic to Jean's outwardly calm exterior. She had only the name of their destination and not a clue as to where they should catch the train. Eventually she asked a railway employee, and he took her by the hand, seized the suitcase and told them to follow him quickly. The train they required was just about to leave, and there would not be another one for several hours.

Dashing down the platform, they almost fell into the train with their suitcase hurled in behind them. The train started to leave immediately, and the man shouted instructions as to where they should change, but his voice was lost in the noise and confusion and Jean could not hear. She now found herself worrying not about which train to get on, but when to get off. David said he felt sure the man had said the train would split at one point, but he had no idea which section they had to be on. At this point Jean could scarcely remember the name of their final destination, she was in such a state.

Looking up, she was astonished to see a man sitting opposite them. She could have sworn the carriage was empty when they had scrambled in, or they would have trampled over him in the rush. How on earth had he avoided the suitcase being hurled at their feet after them? It was all very strange. The man smiled and exuded calmness as he said, 'Please do not worry, I will help.' Jean felt instantly relaxed.

The train passed through some very beautiful countryside and Jean, who was passionately fond of trees, found herself thinking how lovely they were. The man smiled at her and said, 'Yes, they are lovely aren't they,' as if answering a question, although Jean had not spoken her thought.

Thirty minutes after leaving Euston, the man put his newspaper down and said, 'You must get off at the next stop and join the front half of the train.' He then told them the name of the final destination where they should alight. Unquestioningly, Jean stepped from the train at the next stop. Taking their suitcase, the man followed them down the platform. They seemed to be in the middle of nowhere, Jean thought, not a station at all – just an open platform with fields on either side. The platform was quite long, and it was a fair walk to the front of the long train.

Seeing them safely onto the train, the man

reminded Jean of the name of the station where she should alight. The thought went through Jean's head that how on earth did he know where they were going when she did not herself? Closing the door behind them, Jean turned to say thank you to the kind man. She put her head through the window, but to her amazement there was no-one there. The long platform was empty, yet there was nowhere he could possibly have gone in only seconds, with no buildings in sight.

Jean and David stared at each other and slowly added up the events. They were certain the man had not been in the train carriage when they had got in. Where had he come from? He seemed to have the ability to read Jean's thoughts. How? He knew without being told where they must change and where they were going. What on earth had happened? Safely reaching their final destination, they were relieved to find their friends waiting for them. Jean was asked by her friends if something had happened, because they both had such a glow about them. Jean answered, 'It's no wonder we're glowing. We've just met an angel.'

O ur final mystery takes place in Northumberland and centres around Henrietta. For forty years Henrietta had lived in a very large old

house. It had belonged to her husband's family and they had moved in the week they had been married. Children had been born and grown up there, and eventually flown the nest. When Henrietta's husband died, she knew sooner or later she would have to make a painful decision. It was all too obvious that she could not live in the large old house alone. It was far too big for one person to manage from a practical and financial point of view, and the only logical solution was to move somewhere smaller. After much searching, a manageable cottage was found. It was, if anything, older than Henrietta's house, built of solid grey stone, with a little garden and a view of the hills. Once she had sorted everything out, she knew she would be fine.

Abandoning her large amounts of furniture was heart-rending but necessary. Eventually all was ready, and the day of the move dawned. Her family rallied round and jollied her along as the removal van was filled. The move would be a distance of only ten miles or so, and she thought it would be an easy matter to visit old neighbours. The family working party soon had everything safely installed in the cottage. There was a sprinkling of snow on the hills, and the view was breathtaking. Spring would bring surprises of discovering what appeared in the garden, and it would be marvellous to see the cherry tree bloom.

It was getting late, and at last her family said goodnight. The bed was ready in the bedroom, but Henrietta was so tired she felt she could have fallen asleep on the floor. She had a sound night's sleep, and thought that a good omen. The following morning, taking a shower and dressing, she told herself that she was very lucky, but deep down she realised she was whistling in the dark. There was a real sense of loss that she was trying to ignore, and a rising fear that she would regret her actions.

By the time she was ready to descend the stairs, she felt all optimism drain away and a gloom descend. Close to tears, she slowly made her way downstairs. Stepping from the last step, she looked up and was startled to see a young boy standing in the hall. She guessed him to be about ten years old, and he appeared to be dressed in a large, white, Victorian nightshirt. There was an inner glow coming from this child, and he beamed broadly at Henrietta.

She could not move, but stood rooted to the spot, staring in incredulity. In the blink of an eye he was gone, but he had left an atmosphere of such happiness and love that Henrietta wanted to cry with joy. What could this mean? Who was this child? Finally Henrietta decided that he was an angel, reassuring her that all would be well and that happiness would surround her in her new home.

She has not seen the boy again, but she was absolutely right about the reassurance. She is most definitely extremely happy in her lovely old cottage.

Epilogue

Some people think children are naïve, limited by their youth and inexperience. I hope these stories will demonstrate that, on the contrary, children often have a wisdom beyond their years. Whereas adults are often blinkered by their rational minds, children tend to operate out of their unfettered intuition and open hearts. This enables them to perceive directly manifestations of the unseen world, unclouded by prejudice and preconceptions.

In this book we have seen a great variety of angelic appearances and manifestations. Although angels often seem to appear in the form of a traditional 'church angel' with long white robe and wings, surrounded by an aura or glow of light, they may also appear very small in size, or in contemporary dress, sometimes even without wings. Quite often they appear in the form of a dead friend or relative, especially when their purpose is to reassure the child that the dead person is now safe, happy, whole – and still connected to the child. They have always been associated with beauty, and are often accompanied by heavenly music or exquisite scents. Sometimes a waft of roses – when there are no flowers in the room – may be the only sign of their presence.

Angels have many functions. They visit children to comfort them in their loneliness, suffering, sickness and bereavement. Guardian angels rescue children from near-certain death, at times when their human guardians are helpless to intervene. They aid sick children in the healing process, sometimes helping them towards a miraculous recovery when doctors and nurses have given up hope. Sadly, there are times when children do die, but angels are often there to strengthen them in their final hours, and to comfort their bereaved family. Children sometimes have more faith than their parents that a sick friend or relation will recover, because they have received an angelic communication.

Angels often act in mysterious ways, and there is no telling who will be graced by a visitation. As we have sometimes seen, they do not visit only in emergencies, but at any moment in our lives, sometimes out of the blue and for no apparent reason at all. They seem to be attracted by abounding joy almost as much as by grief and fear. Visits at such times may make as profound an impression on a child's life as rescue from an accident.

Why do angels visit children, or indeed adults? There are many theories, and nobody knows for sure. What does seem certain, from these and other stories, is that they always have a positive and inspirational purpose. An angelic visit is clearly remembered for a lifetime, even when it took place in early childhood and the person has reached old age. They give children comfort, consolation, and the courage to continue a life that may be hard, painful, full of challenge. As we have seen, they also often give children a sense of purpose in their lives, which may not be revealed until adulthood. This purpose often seems connected with creative expression or helping and inspiring others in some way.

My hope is that readers of these inspiring stories will receive comfort and hope for their own lives. Angelic manifestations can help us make sense of certain puzzling, perhaps half-forgotten, experiences in our lives, when we may have felt touched by an inexplicably unseen presence. They can also reassure us that we are not alone in a cold, hostile universe. We all have guardian angels who watch over and protect us, and who may well make themselves known to us at the right moment.

If you have had an angel experience and would be willing to share it with the author, please contact her at New Church College, 25 Radcliffe New Road, Radcliffe, Manchester M26 1LE.

Also available from Rider:

AN ANGEL AT MY SHOULDER
True Stories of Angelic Experiences
Glennyce S. Eckersley

An Angel At My Shoulder shows angels are returning — and being acknowledged — once again. Here are true stories of countless ordinary people being rescued by angels, being comforted and healed by them, feeling their presence in the face of death — and often appearing to little children. These tales are drawn from such countries as Britain, Australia, Ireland and the United States — showing angels can be found all round the globe: helping others, often changing their lives completely.

Warm and uplifting, *An Angel At My Shoulder* suggests it is more than time to reconsider our view of angels, to let them back into our hectic, mechanized world and to realise we are never alone . . .

'If you believe in angels Glennyce S. Eckersley's extraordinary true stories about angelic encounters will affirm your belief that angels are truly watching over us. If you don't believe in angels, you may find your non-belief wavering . . . This book touches the soul and opens the doors to the realm where heaven and earth meet and love abounds.'

DENISE LINN, author of *Sacred Space*

OUT OF THE BLUE
Modern-Day Miracles & Extraordinary Coincidences
Glennyce S. Eckersley

This book is about coincidences and modern-day miracles: the seemingly random acts that may well turn out to be not so random after all. How do they happen? – why? – and to whom?

Only in recent times have we felt alone and isolated in our universe. Yet for centuries men and women fervently believed in the intervention of a higher power in their lives. Today, as more of us search for greater spiritual fulfilment, we wonder once again whether such events might mean we live, not in a purely chaotic world, but rather in one of harmony, meaning and order at a deeper level.

Glennyce S. Eckersley has here collected many extraordinary true stories of coincidences in the everyday, in nature and in dreams – as well as spiritual stories and contemporary miracles from around the globe. All of these suggest the many different things that happen to us must be fundamentally interconnected and meaningful – though they so often appear straight *out of the blue*.

PROUD SPIRIT
Lessons, Insights & Healing from the Voice of the Spirit World
Rosemary Altea

In this extraordinary book, Rosemary Altea explores opportunities for spiritual growth in our everyday experiences. Using stories from her work and also from her personal life, she answers such questions as: Will our human personalities survive death intact? Are people in the spirit world affected by the actions of their loved ones on earth?

But this remarkable *tour de force* goes well beyond the subject of life after death, presenting awe-inspiring tales that shine a light on human conduct, such as the spine-tingling visit of children from the spirit world – or the story of an abused young boy who is kept safe by his guardian angel.

Hopeful, uplifting, strengthening, Rosemary Altea challenges us to know, value and be gentle with ourselves – to be *proud spirits*.

If you would like to order any of the following or to receive our catalogue please fill in the form below:

An Angel At My Shoulder by Glennyce S. Eckersley £6.99
Out of the Blue by Glennyce S. Eckersley £6.99
Proud Spirit by Rosemary Altea £6.99
Sacred Space by Denise Linn £6.99
Feng Shui for the Soul by Denise Linn £12.99
The Five Stages of the Soul by Harry R. Moody and David Carroll £6.99
The Rebirth of Nature by Rupert Sheldrake £9.99
The Seat of the Soul by Gary Zukav £10.99
Animals as Teachers and Healers by Susan Chernak McElroy £8.99
Optimum Healing by Dr. Craig Brown £9.99
The Projection of the Astral Body by Sylvan Muldoon and Hereward Carrington £10.99
The Little Book of Inner Space by Stafford Whiteaker £1.99
The Little Book of Happiness by Patrick Whiteside £1.99

HOW TO ORDER

BY POST: TBS Direct, TBS Ltd, Colchester Road, Frating Green, Essex CO7 7DW

Please send me _____ copies of _____ @ £_____ each

☐ I enclose my cheque for £ _____ payable to Rider Books

☐ Please charge £ _____ to my American Express/Visa/Mastercard account* *(*delete as applicable*)*

Card No ☐☐☐☐☐☐☐☐☐☐☐☐☐☐☐☐

Expiry Date: ☐☐☐☐ Signature _____

Name _____

Address _____

_____ Postcode _____

Delivery address if different _____

_____ Postcode _____

Or call our credit card hotline on 01206 255800.

Please have your card details handy.

Please quote reference: Chilfing

Rider is an imprint of Random House UK Ltd
Please tick here if you do not wish to receive further information from Rider or associated companies ☐